The Real Estate Agent's Business Planning Guide

. . . .

Carla Cross

Real Estate
Education Company
a division of Dearborn Financial Publishing, Inc.

While a great deal of care has been taken to provide accurate and current information, the ideas, suggestions, general principles and conclusions presented in this text are subject to local, state and federal laws and regulations, court cases and any revisions of same. The reader is thus urged to consult legal counsel regarding any points of law—this publication should not be used as a substitute for competent legal advice.

Publisher: Kathleen A. Welton
Managing Editor: Jack L. Kiburz
Associate Editor: Karen A. Christensen
Interior Design: Professional Resources & Communications, Inc.
Cover Design: Taccone Art & Design

Printed in the United States of America

94 95 96 10 9 8 7 6 5 4 3 2 1

Library of Congress Cataloging-in-Publication Data

Cross, Carla
     The real estate agent's business planning guide / by Carla Cross.
        p.   cm.
     Includes bibliographical references (p.   ) and index.
     ISBN 0-79310-955-8 (pbk.)
     1. Real estate business—Planning—Handbooks, manuals, etc. 2. Real estate agents. I. Title.
HD1375.C683 1994   94-13219
333.33'068'4—dc20   CIP

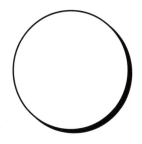

Dedication

. . . .

To my family, for their unconditional support. Thank you, Dick and Chris!

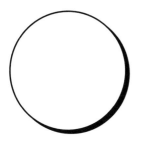

Acknowledgments

· · · · · · · · · · · · · · · · · · · ·

Many thanks to all the agents and managers who proved that this system works:

- The agents in my East Bellevue office, who, through working with me as I evolved the system, helped refine and clarify the approach.
- The agents in my West Seattle office, who use this business planning approach to plan a highly profitable business, and who showed me that, with the directions in this book, agents can create a dynamic plan.

Many thanks to the hundreds of students who have learned this process in my business planning courses. They have shown me what works—and what's simple and effective.

A special thanks to my terrific assistant, Teresa Lindbloom, for her support during this project.

To Patrick Hogan, acquisitions editor, a personal acknowledgment for his expert advice on content, balance and marketing.

I am confident that, whether you're an agent, manager or trainer, you can quickly put the principles of this system to work for you—for greater productivity and profitability.

With best wishes for your success,
Carla Cross, CRB

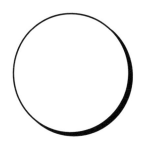

Contents

· · · · · · · · · · · · · · · · · · · ·

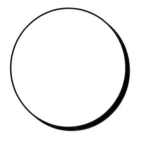

Preface

Business planning for real estate agents is not a new concept. Real estate agents have heard the term business planning for years. From examples that I gathered as I taught business planning workshops across the United States, I discovered that a business plan may be anything from a one-page, goal-setting sheet to a narrative description of how agents intend to conduct business. A comparison of these planning systems to the business planning processes used by other industries shows that what has been termed business planning for the real estate industry falls short. To assure that agents receive the same benefits from the planning process as any business owner, real estate plans should provide:

- a system that encompasses all the major considerations any business owner must weigh—after all, agents are business owners; and

- a process that teaches us how to *think* about our business.

As important as systems and processes are, there's one other benefit a great planning system provides: It is detailed and practical enough to actually tell agents what to do each day. Having worked with this particular business planning system for years, I believe that it provides the kind of specific guidance an agent needs to be successful. Agents who have used the plan tell me that this planning system gets down to where "the rubber meets the road." Recently, as I was teaching a business planning workshop, a few experienced, successful agents remarked, "We have all heard about business planning for the last few years, but your course helped us make sense of it. You helped us relate planning concepts to what we do every day to ensure our success as real estate salespeople."

In writing this book, I have a rather grand vision. My purpose is not merely to show you another planning system, but to provide you with the tools to craft a better business for yourself. To be practical and valuable, a good plan should have built-in systems to help you jump the hurdles as you strive to grow your career. From my two decades of real estate practice, I've identified three major challenges to an agent's career growth:

1. Managing time for maximum production
2. Recognizing productive business patterns and correcting unproductive ones
3. Making the right marketing moves for your career pace

Managing Your Time. It's a misnomer. We do not manage time; we manage activities. The root of an agent's time management problems lies in the fact that many agents don't understand their job description; that is, they do not know exactly which activities they should accomplish each day to give them the pay-off—a commission check. Through agents' real-life stories, planning grids and guidelines, this book helps you get on track and stay on track:

A real estate salesperson finds prospects who want to purchase homes. He qualifies prospects, shows prospects and sells them homes. A real estate salesperson also finds prospects who want to sell their homes. He qualifies prospects and lists clients' homes until those homes are sold.

Notice that *people*—that is, prospects, buyers and sellers—are intrinsic to the activities that real estate salespeople complete. Interestingly, though, many activities that agents complete during their business days do not involve people who will buy or sell with the agent. Instead, the activities involve *things*—seeing homes, doing market analyses, following up, completing paperwork, attending meetings or classes. When an agent's job description (daily activity plan) gets top-heavy with things, the agent fails in real estate. Part of the responsibility of any good planning system is to get the people back into the agent's cycle of activities. With the unique planning worksheets in this book, you'll automatically put people first in your plan.

Building on Your Successes—and Eliminating Your Mistakes. Successful business owners look for patterns of their success, so that they can repeat the pattern. They honestly address their mistakes, so that they can eliminate them. Unfortunately, most real estate planning systems offer few methods to help you accomplish this analysis. However, this planning system devotes one entire chapter to analyzing your business. Discovering what's right and what's wrong is important to know if you want to save money and effort the next year. Obviously, you will want to keep doing more of what worked! For example, using the worksheets in the internal research section, you will discover where your business came from—that is your best market to target next year. You will be able to build a marketing plan to exploit that particular market. You will also find what is promotable about your business and be able to build effective personal promotional campaigns.

Not only will you find, from your internal analysis, what you did right, you will discover mistakes to avoid in the future. One of the most common mistakes is that agents list too many properties that do not sell. This business practice results in money thrown down the drain and high levels of customer dissatisfaction. With their past statistics as benchmarks, agents can build a better plan to correct this mistake and become more profitable—with no increase in effort or expenses.

The Right Personal Marketing Moves for You. Agents have great difficulty choosing the marketing moves that are appropriate for their career stage—and no wonder. Today, it seems that everybody is on the seminar trail telling agents how to promote themselves. The problem is that agents have no frame of reference—they do not know how to fit all these great ideas into their business lives. The chapter on personal marketing, which relates personal marketing principles to each agent's stage in his career, solves this problem for agents. By reading the chapter and working with the planning worksheets, you can select the personal marketing moves that will propel you to your goals, while saving money.

This book will help you choose the right career moves. Most agents are not yet superstars raking in the bucks. They are still building their careers. This book provides dozens of examples about how agents in career growth can employ marketing tactics that are relevant to their career stages and budgets. It gives dozens of examples of agents, like you, who have put these guidelines to work. My objective is to help you create yourself so vividly and authentically that you'll be able to choose the right marketing moves for you—with confidence and creativity.

Planning and Management Concepts for the 21st Century. To assure that you are capturing the best of the future in your plan, I integrated some contemporary planning and management concepts into this system. I incorporated concepts such as *strategic intent, core competency, total customer satisfaction, total quality management* and *spider-web management style* into this planning system. By following the processes in this book, you will be managing yourself and others with the newest business planning and management concepts.

The System Works. As an agent, manager and trainer, I spent almost a decade creating and refining this particular planning system. I used it in my first management position to help agents become first in per-agent productivity in a 19-office company. I use it in my present office and, as a result, have doubled production in one year and doubled the ratio of listings taken to listings sold. *What a time management concept!* Besides my own results, I have been gratified with the comments from agents and managers nationwide who have learned the system. For example, Nancy Colson, associate broker, comments: "This kind of guidance is much needed in our industry. With this planning process, I have been able to focus my time and activities on those things that are most productive and make the most sense for my business."

Managers, too, get rewards from working with their agents in this system. Jan Johnson, real estate office owner, commented: "I want to let you know about the positive actions as a result of learning your system. We spent our last sales meeting reviewing and sharing some results from the class. It's helped us focus on productive activities and brought our group together."

Improvise!   We all go into real estate with big dreams and expectations. This book provides a concrete process to make your dreams become business reality. We all bring our unique and diverse life experiences to real estate. At age four, for some reason, I crawled up on a piano bench and started playing the piano. I went on to attain two degrees in music. When I started selling real estate, I thought I had gone to another planet! However, I found that there were many parallels between musical performance and real estate sales. I started seeing selling as a performance art—similar to musical performance. After all, it's not what we know, but what we do (perform) that ensures our success. From my jazz background, I realize that I must know the tune before I can improvise. This planning system provides you a 'tune'—the basic planning structure. But, the fun of planning comes in creating your improvisations—your unique marketing moves and professional development strategies. *The Real Estate Agent's Business Planning Guide* will give you the structure and the flexibility you need to create with confidence.

In my "former life," I was working with a brilliant percussionist who had played vibes with George Shearing. Sometimes when we were ready to begin a complex jazz piece, I would literally freeze in fear. Doug would turn to me and say, "Straight ahead and strive for tone." In other words, just start. That's my advice to you. After only a few months of working with this system, your business will improve. Your attitude will become increasingly professional. You will be using the systems and processes that ensure a dynamic, successful real estate career. Congratulations on beginning this exciting process!

CHAPTER

The Concept of
Business Planning

"There's no reason why anyone cannot do well in real estate following this plan. I know firsthand this system works."

—**Nada Sundermeyer**

In This Chapter •

Why plan?

Who needs a plan?

What's in a plan?

How is this system different?

Why Plan?

You just received an unexpected but welcome $10,000 bonus. You want to spend it on the trip of your dreams. How do you decide where to go, what to see, how to spend your money?

As you read that first sentence, you probably thought about all the places that you would like to see. You mulled over the possibilities for your trip, compared the pros and cons of various countries, then narrowed your choices. You made your final choice and considered what you would do in that country, how many days to spend in each city, mementos to buy—the special decisions that would make experiences you would treasure for a lifetime. If you ever planned a special trip, you know that planning is a pleasure in itself. You also know that you enjoy the trip more if the planning is done well. You would not dream of taking a trip that costs you $10,000

1

without some extensive planning. The point is that, when we look forward to a valuable, pleasurable experience, taking time to plan is normal—and *the planning process is pleasurable.*

However, when agents relate planning to their own businesses, they sometimes attach different feelings to the planning process. Many real estate agents look at planning as a "have to." They do it because their managers tell them they must "set some goals" or "have a business plan." Planning because you think you have to is an exercise in futility. As an agent, I always resented goal-setting because I could not relate it to my "real" real estate life. Setting income goals just did not seem to relate to what I was doing every day. At the end of the year, I dutifully gave my manager my "goals"—those numbers that I thought would light up his eyes! Then I forgot about the discussion and went about my business. I attained recognition as one of the ten top agents in my 400-agent company. But imagine what I could have done with a well-defined plan.

Who Needs a Plan?

Sometimes people try to pass the responsibility of planning to someone else. Recently, at a meeting of a local professional organization, someone asked whether the organization had a plan. The local president replied, "The national organization has a plan. We do not need a plan." Can you guess what happened to that local organization? That's right. Not much!

But what about real estate agents? Their companies have plans. So why do agents need business plans? Without a plan that relates to an agent's daily activities, he or she does not know what to do each day. A company's plan simply will not provide the specific direction to the people involved that will get them from start to finish.

It's Not the Plan's Fault

Have you known people who created the most divine plans but failed miserably? Was it the plan or the person? The point of planning is not to prove that you can write a good plan following the guidelines! Planning simply provides a thought process that will *get you into action quickly, while saving time, effort and money. The proof of a good plan lies in the results of the actions.*

Thinking about Planning

Pretend that you are the author of a best-seller. Hollywood has asked you to create a movie based on that best-seller. You are thrilled and immediately start creating a movie script to be sure that your book "comes alive" on the big screen. There is one problem—you have never created a movie script. However, since you visualized the novel as you wrote it, you easily translate the words, scenes, feelings, smells and sounds to a movie script. The more precisely you envision this movie, the better the script—and the better the movie will be.

Think of planning your real estate career in the same way. You have been living your real estate life. In fact, if you are like most of us, you have said that your experiences could make a best-selling novel! If you had recorded this life, you would have a finished movie of your career to date. Now, you want to create a new script—a movie that will star you as a successful real estate salesperson. Your planning process creates your movie. The more you think about the movie, the more precisely you plan it, the better the movie will be. Then all you need to do is to "live" this movie in your real estate career. Thinking of planning as moviemaking gives an entirely different view to goal-setting. As an agent, my problem with goal-setting was that it was not precise enough. Although I stated my desired end result, I had no plan for exactly how to achieve the results. I had no movie script. In the planning process provided in this book, you will create not only the end result you want, but exactly how you intend to get there—a complete movie script so that you can see yourself in the actions that guarantee your success.

What's Real

According to psychologists, the mind cannot differentiate between a vividly imagined event and an event that actually happened. You know the feeling. You are watching a movie, and, even though you *know* it is only a movie, you find yourself reacting as though you were in the scene! Thus, it seems logical that, if you create a well-imagined movie of yourself as a successful real estate salesperson, you will take the actions in your real estate career that portray you that way. A well-thought-out plan provides that precise movie.

Psychologists have also discovered that, if your movie is more vivid in your mind than your reality, you believe the movie rather than the reality. Thus, if you want to change your career toward greater success, make a better movie (through planning) than your previous (your past career). As you play the new movie over in your mind, you will probably find that you like your new role better than the previous. Then you make the movie come true in your real estate actions. Martha, an agent in my office, made $28,000 her third year in business. During our planning conference, Martha expressed dissatisfaction with her level of income. She had always been a high achiever and compared herself to other agents making $100,000 a year. She felt she was more like them than like a $28,000-a-year salesperson, yet her income did not prove it! What was happening to Martha? The original movie of Martha as a real estate salesperson was being replaced by a better movie—one that portrayed her as she had always seen herself. But how would Martha flesh out the details of the new movie? Working together through her business planning process, using the planning system in this book, Martha and I created a plan for her that assured her of attaining the goals in her new movie—$100,000. Admittedly, that's a huge leap—from $28,000 to $100,000. Beware of making big leaps without precise planning and lots of motivation to achieve. Martha was so motivated, and her plan was so strong, that she attained her goal. And she has been in the top one percent of the agents in the 800-agent company ever since.

What's in a Plan?

Let's go back to planning for that trip of a lifetime. The planning process for the trip is the same process that businesses use. A good planning system consists of four steps (see Figure 1.1), in this order:

1. *Assess the situation.*   In a process commonly used by international corporations, this step is called *situation analysis*. During this first phase, the planner gathers all the data needed to make good planning decisions. When our son Chris was asked to participate in an international karate tournament in Hungary a few years ago, we were initially excited about his opportunity. But before giving our consent, we gathered information. Unfortunately at the time, plane hijacking was common, especially on the air routes to Budapest. We decided that it would be better for Chris not to go. Gathering adequate data is a very important part of planning, a part that is commonly left out of many planning systems. With this system, you will gather critical data to help you make the best decisions about your career moves.

2. *Define your business focus.*   Also referred to as defining your mission, vision or strategic intent, this step helps you to define how you fit into the picture you created during your situation analysis—the picture of the real estate business. In a movie, this would be the character's traits and motives. What is your business focus? How do you see yourself? When agents do not take the time to create a business focus, they can waste considerable time and money on inappropriate activities. For example: As a new agent, no one told me about planning, much less defining my business focus. I thought I was a "generic" real estate salesperson, who could—and should—

sell real estate over the entire state of Washington. After all, my license said I could! So I listed two lots on a river 100 miles from my office. That was sure an exercise in futility. I did not know the area, I could not find the lots—I dreaded that someone would want to see them! Obviously, I did not get any more business in that area. And I certainly did not provide customer service! If I had created a business focus for myself at the beginning of my career, I would have realized I needed to turn down some business so that I could focus my efforts in a defined area—and become known as an area expert.

Because I did not have a clear picture of myself in my real estate world, I worked in areas and with people who did not benefit my real estate career. Unfortunately, I had to learn all this from the "school of hard knocks." Following the planning process outlined in this book can save you energy, time and money.

3. *Decide on the end results you want.* Most planning processes call these *objectives.* These are the goals—the end results—that you want to attain. Martha changed her end results from $28,000 to $100,000. After a thorough analysis of all the research gathered in the first step of the planning process, and after putting yourself into the picture you created with that research, you can decide on your end results.

4. *Decide what you will do and how you will do it to attain these results.* In many planning processes, the "whats" are called *strategies.* The "hows" are called *tactics.* Because I have seen considerable confusion when planners try to differentiate between a strategy and a tactic, I will discuss these categories together. The point is that, in order to create a movie, the scriptwriter must decide what the characters will do, when they will do it, and how they will do it. A good planning system helps the planner decide exactly how he wants to "act" to get the desired results. During this part of the planning process, planners assign duties to themselves and others. They create budgets for the activities. They attach time frames to start and end the activities. In addition, planners create a way to measure the success of the activities. The planner precisely defines the activities so that they can be put into a daily planner and acted on. *Being very detailed in this step is a secret to a successful plan.* The problem with old-style goal-setting is that it gives the planner no method to define or relate those goals to daily activities. That is like telling someone to create a great movie—without a script for the characters to follow.

Figure 1.1

The Four Steps in Planning

1. Assess the situation.

2. Define your business focus.

3. Decide on the end results you want.

4. Decide what you will do and how you will do it to attain these results.

The Evolution of This Planning System

When I started managing an office, I realized that I needed to create an office plan. Through courses that led to my *Certified Real Estate Broker* (CRB) designation (see Appendix A for more information), I learned how to plan using the *strategic planning model*. My first office plan was difficult to write and, in retrospect, not very good. But through continuing the process and involving the agents in our office, I learned to write a plan that worked. I credit this process with the success our office enjoyed: First in per-agent productivity and profitability in a company of 19 offices. Most importantly, I learned how to adapt the strategic planning model to the real estate office planning process. More information on this adaptation can be found in Chapter 10.

After writing plans for the office, I tackled the job of adapting this planning process to fit an agent's needs. Again, my first efforts needed improvement. But, after eight years of using and adapting this process, I have created a system that works well for the agents that I manage. In addition, for the past five years, I have taught a two-day workshop across the country to help agents understand and use this system. My one-day course for managers based on this system is now offered nationally as part of the CRB series. It is sponsored by the Real Estate Brokerage Managers' Council, an affiliate of the National Association of REALTORS® (NAR). See the Reference section.

How This Planning System Is Different

Focus on Profitability. When I started selling real estate, the company and I evenly split the total commission dollars that came into the company as a result of my sales efforts. The company planned, budgeted and spent its money on various marketing tactics to bring business to me. I did not have to plan, allocate and budget much of my own commission dollars to create business. Today, the opposite is true. Because agents capture more of the gross commission dollar, they must manage their dollars as though they were a business. Truly, now they are a business within a business.

We all know it takes money to make money. In the '90s much of the burden of planning, budgeting and allocating funds to create and re-create business is on the agent. If they are not careful, agents can end up spending more dollars than they make. They may spend money in ways that do not pay off. Or they may not spend enough money to create business, because they do not realize that things have changed. Old-style planning systems focused the agent on *productivity*. Because agents need to spend more of their own money today, a good planning system must help them focus on *profitability*.

In this planning system, you will assign costs to each of your marketing tactics, prepare an overall budget and plan your budget over time. Then you will plot your income, subtract your expenses and discover your projected profit. I have created straightforward, easily completed forms to help you project and keep track of your income, expenses and profit. Knowing ahead of time the cost of a promotional project will help you project your expected results and make a decision about whether you want to launch into that particular promotional project.

"Fail-Safe" Features Are Built In. This is not just another planning system. Within this plan, there are many safety nets: Processes, systems and tips that can save agents time, money and effort. Through ten years of evolving this system, I know the pitfalls agents can experience in the planning process. I have made every effort to ensure that, as you go through this planning process, you will develop thought patterns that will ensure a good plan—a plan that will deliver the success you expect in this business.

As you create your plan, I will point out areas to watch for and ways to evaluate each part of your plan. I will provide examples to make the planning process pleasurable. All you need to do is to get into action; the plan will get you where you want to go.

It Works.   Real estate agents are a cynical lot. They like to know that things work "in the real world," that other people have been successful using certain methods. This planning system has worked for hundreds of agents *in their worlds.*

With this easily accomplished process, you can create the specific activities that match your talents and aspirations—your business focus. It is built around your specific world—your market conditions, your company, your office. Instead of listing the ten activities you always ought to do, this planning system provides the process to *make the activity choices that are appropriate for you.* And, finally, this planning system outlines the process to help you reassess, evaluate and make the changes in your plan to create even greater success. In other words, *the power is in the process.*

How To Use This Book

First, scan through the chapters in *The Real Estate Agent's Business Planning Guide* to get an idea of how the system works. Then go back through each section and complete the worksheets.

Major Point

 When you see this symbol, pay particular attention. It alerts you to an important concept or strategy—one that can affect the success of your system as you create it.

When You're Finished

Use the checklist in Chapter 11 (see Figure 11.7) to be sure that you have integrated all the critical concepts into your plan.

Sample Business Plan

In Appendix A there are examples of two agents' plans:

1. An agent with less than one year's experience who wants to establish a fast-growing career

2. An agent who wants to grow his career to high profitability

Planning Worksheets

A set of blank planning worksheets (see Appendix B) illustrate the "bare bones" of the process. Managers and agents can use these in their planning sessions.

How This System Is Organized

Literally dozens of ways to organize a business plan exist. By using various organizations during the past ten years, I found a particular system that is simple, concise and applicable to a real estate agent's business. The system consists of three steps (see Figure 1.2):

1. *Research* your market, your prior business and your competitors.
2. Create your *focusing statement.*
3. Write your *action plan.* It is divided into two parts: the *marketing section* and the *professional development section* (see Figure 1.3). Much of your planning focuses on creating a marketing plan—one that will expand your business opportunities. When you do market research, you are gathering critical information that directly affects your marketing decisions. As you create your focusing statement, you are making an overall marketing strategy for yourself. In the marketing world, this is called *positioning.* (See Chapter 4 for more about focusing.) After you have gathered information and decided on your focus, you can create the action steps to create and expand your businesses. This system provides a unique, yet easy method to choose the best markets in which to expand your business. In addition, this system offers a creative, effective method that will help you organize your actions to ensure that you get a "bigger bang for the buck."

Developing and Supporting You

In addition to marketing, you need to develop other parts of your business. When you look at your listings in the research phase, you may discover that you sold only 40 percent of the listings you took. To better use your time, you may decide to increase it to 80 percent. You will set a goal and list the action steps needed to accomplish this conversion rate. In the professional development section of your plan, you will decide how to become more effective and efficient in your business. You will create action moves (tactics) to streamline your business. Figure 1.3 lists the kinds of decisions you will make in each of these action categories.

Figure 1.2

The Three Steps
in This Planning System

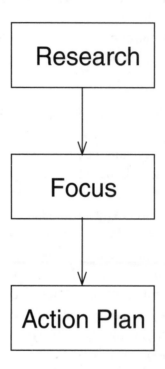

Summary

Planning can be fun and exciting if you view it as an adventurous trip. Making a movie of the best "you" creates a strong picture that draws you to move toward it. The planning process in this book helps you create a precise focus for your movie. As director and star, you will have all the pages of the script that you need to create a vibrant, successful and exciting real estate career.

Figure 1.3

The Action Plan

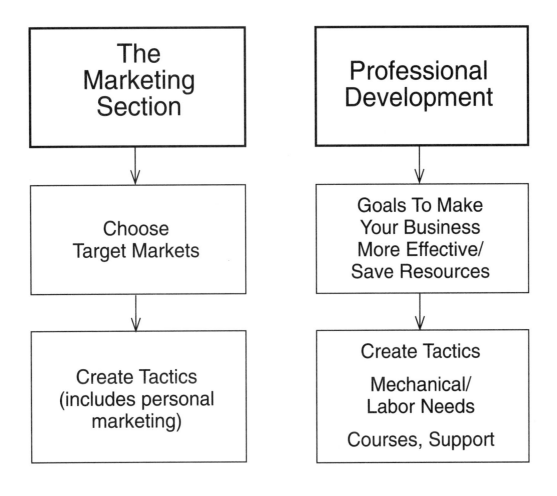

CHAPTER

Reviewing Your Marketplace

"Gathering information from your marketplace and continually tracking activities against results will help you do the most productive thing every given moment."

—Karen Lavellee

In This Chapter ·

Why review?

The two parts of the review

Your market analysis

Why Review?

By reviewing your past business, you can avoid costly mistakes that accrue when you use the same strategies and tactics that worked in the past—but will not work in a different market. Without taking a look at market trends, you cannot adjust your strategies in a timely fashion.

A few years ago, I met with a company's 15 top agents to help them create a business plan using this system. All these agents were multimillion dollar producers, and about three-quarters of them conducted most of their business with builders and planned to continue to do so. Following the process in this system, we started with a review that included the inventory of available lots. We estimated development costs, and with this information, we concluded that lots would double in the next year. Therefore, the total package price of a home and lot would be out of reach for most of our purchasers. Based on this information, the agents adjusted their plans and switched their businesses back in resale, emphasizing recontacting past customers and clients. They were very successful that next year, while agents in other companies who continued to represent builders made less money.

A Common Planning Mistake

Agent planners often make the mistake of skipping the review step. Why? They may not understand that analyzing the past allows them to make much more accurate plans for the future. Or perhaps their previous planning system did not have a section devoted to review. However, I have found that taking time to assess statistics, identify trends and analyze information helps me chart a course that will ensure my success. Agents often ask: "Which marketing methods are best?" "How can I spend my money in ways that always work?" These questions and concerns can only be answered with a detailed, specific *situation analysis*—an analysis of the market conditions that affect that particular agent.

A good review helps agents make good tactical choices—the specific actions they decide will get them to their objectives. Without an adequate review, agents tend to reject good ideas, saying, "It will not work for me in my area." The idea of the review is to get the analytical perspective to *translate* ideas that worked for someone else to you and your area.

The Two Parts of the Review

Because this part of the plan is so important, I have dedicated two chapters to it. This chapter looks at the "external" picture. Chapter 3 focuses on your business. The review is divided into two parts (see Figure 2.1):

1. *Your market analysis* provides a review of the trends, opportunities and challenges of the market, as determined by the political, economic and geographic climates in your market area. It also includes an analysis of your company's strengths and challenges, along with your best competitor's strengths and challenges.

2. *Your business* provides a review of your prospecting methods, transactions, business methods and skills. Also included is a personal internal analysis.

With an in-depth understanding of your markets and your personal businesses, you can create dynamic power plays—moves in your business that launch you ahead of the pack—with the security of knowing that you are dedicating your resources in the right directions.

Figure 2.1

The Review

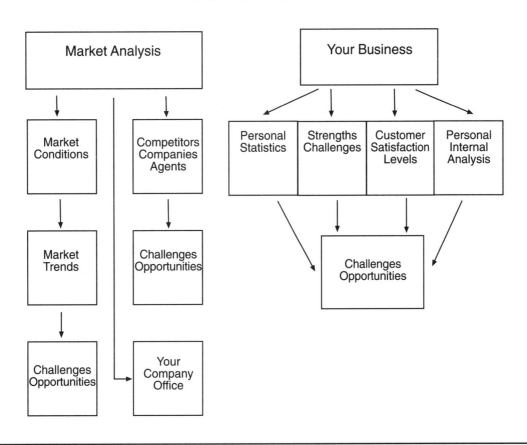

The Big Picture

The first step, *market analysis*, starts with a review of your larger business environment. The point of the analysis is to draw together facts, statistics and information that indicate trends. Then you can recognize the challenges you face in your business and the opportunities that you can take advantage of. Figure 2.2 provides a checklist for your big-picture market review.

Market Analysis

When I started selling real estate, I thought my job was simply to find buyers and sellers. I did not recognize the impact of market conditions upon my business. However, I soon discovered that a certain area condition greatly impacted how I should conduct my business. I started selling real

Figure 2.2

The Big Picture

Evaluate these factors as you believe they impact your market:
+   Positive Impact
-    Negative Impact
o   No Impact

	Rating	Comments

National
      Economy
      Politics
      Environment
      Employment
      National resources
 	
Local
      Economy
      Politics
      Environment
      Mortgage availability
      Consumer interest rates
      Housing availability
      Natural resources
      Schools
      Community services
      Employment		

estate in 1973 in a suburb of Seattle, Washington, at the end of the "Boeing slump." This was a year a billboard on the outskirts of Seattle stated: Will the last one to leave please turn out the lights? There were many more homes available than buyers—known as a *buyer's market*. Agents who were concentrating on listing properties were starving. However, agents who were actively looking for buyers and agents who could arrange creative financing were making a living. I quickly learned to follow the advice of my boss: *Work the market you are given*. I did not know how to do a market analysis or review, but I got the point. You cannot make rates go up or down; you cannot reduce the amount of inventory; but you can choose how to work and who to work with. If you quickly recognize changing market conditions and pinpoint trends, you can adjust your businesses to take advantage of these changes. Unfortunately, many agents take months or years to recognize market changes.

I started managing a real estate office when interest rates were 18 percent (looking back—what an opportunity!). Our company's agents had been taught that "if you don't list, you don't last." So they did much more listing than selling. However, when rates went to 18 percent, none of those listings were selling. Instead of making adjustments in their marketing tactics (such as reducing prices, adding creative financing, searching for buyers), agents complained about the market. Several agents in my office refused to counsel sellers on the changed market conditions because "the sellers needed a higher price for their home." I tried to convince the agents that they could not change the market, but some agents chose to just wait out the market. However, this high interest rate market was not a few months long; the buyer's market lasted for many months.

As you can imagine, agents who did not adjust to changed market conditions had to leave the business. Those few who did adjust were very successful in this market. The key to a successful real estate career is to recognize changes in market conditions as trends and to adjust your business to take advantage of the trends.

Your Market Analysis

After you assess area conditions, narrow your scope to your own market. Use Figure 2.3 to gather your statistics. Adjust the price ranges to fit your market. Your research will help you determine:

- how many homes were on the market. Is this up or down from the previous years?
- how many homes in your market area were sold in the last year. Is this up or down from the previous years?

Figure 2.3

Market Analysis

	This Year	Last Year
Overall Total number of homes available (listed) Total number of homes sold **New** Number of homes available (listed) Number of homes sold **Resale** Number of homes available (listed) Number of homes sold		

By Price Range: Homes Available	This Year	Last Year
0–99		
100–150		
151–200		
201–300		
301–400		
401–500		
over 501		

Figure 2.4

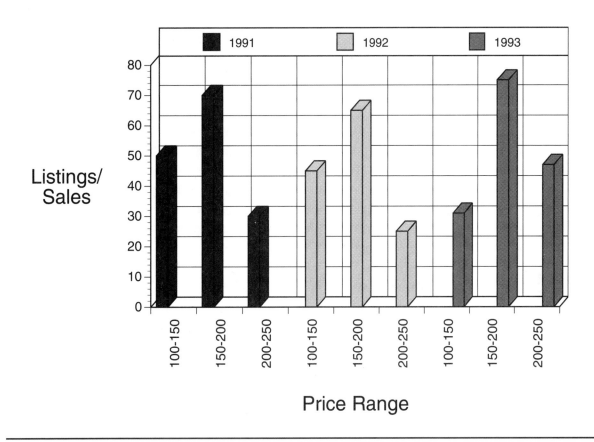

Office Production by Price Range

● the ratio of homes listed to homes sold. Is this up or down from the previous years?

● the ratio of new homes listed and sold to resales listed and sold.

The answers to these questions will indicate whether you are in a seller's market or a buyer's market. Then you can pinpoint how you should conduct your business. Which price ranges were the most active? What is the average time on the market for various price ranges? The answer to these questions indicate the greatest opportunity. Agents who do not conduct this kind of analysis are not aware of the best pockets of opportunity in their markets. Figure 2.4 is a bar chart showing a real estate office's production by price range over a three-year period. You can establish the same kind of trendline to track your business in particular price ranges. By gathering market research and assessing trends yearly, you can target the price ranges of opportunity. Additionally, this information is invaluable to share with sellers.

☞ Sellers need to know market conditions to make good pricing decisions. Using your research in your listing presentation is a powerful tool to add to your credibility.

Analyze Your Company/Your Office

Several of the greatest business opportunities agents have available—but seldom optimize—are the opportunities provided by their companies. What I mean is: Companies spend hundreds of thousands of dollars each year to create support services for agents. But agents, for whatever reason, do not use them. Start thinking about how you can capitalize on the programs created by your company for your use. How well do you understand your company's strengths? What is your company's *core competency*? That is, if I were to ask you what you considered to be the essence of your company—what your company is most competent at—could you pinpoint it? With some companies, it's training. In others, it's marketing.

☞ The more you know about your company, the more effectively you can tie your marketing programs into your company, saving you valuable resources and creating a synergistic marketing effect. Figure 2.5 provides an analysis of your company and office. See your manager to clarify any areas with which you are unfamiliar.

Competitors in Your Marketplace

Picture this. You are in a race, and you are the *only* person in the race. The starting gun gets you on your feet, and you walk at a leisurely pace to the finish line. You win the race. Silly picture, isn't it? Yet, many of us make plans the same way. We decide the moves we will make in our career, as if we had no one competing against us. Go back to that race. Now, imagine that you have five worthy competitors. Your thought process and attitude concerning the race change dramatically. To win that race, you find out all you can about your competitors *before* you hear the starting gun sound. You investigate exactly who the runners are, what their running styles are, and when they like to make their power moves during races. You plan your run with these competitor strategies in mind. And you will need strategies during the race to make adjustments because competitors' positions in a race can *change*.

Think of your career as a race with competitors whose moves constantly change. Not long ago, a group of us reviewed a five-year-old list of leading companies in our market area. Only two out of the ten companies

Figure 2.5

Analyzing Your Company/Your Office

Rate your company / office in these areas:

1 = Highest   2 = Above Average

3 = Average   4 = Needs Improving

	Rating	Comments

Company
    Image/reputation
    Management communication
    Marketing programs
    Training
    Business producing programs
    Team awareness
    Policies
    Creativity
    Compensation
    Planning
 	
Office
    Management
    Support—staff/mechanical
    Team awareness
    Training
    Creativity
    Image
    Working conditions
    Planning
    Communications		

on the list were still owned by the same people. Eight were not in our marketplace or had changed ownership. Without regularly looking at the players, real estate marketers today can get some surprises. A friend of mine calls today's real estate market *white water real estate* because practicing real estate is like shooting the rapids—unpredictable, ever changeable—but exciting!

☞   When assessing your competitors, remember that *their evolution affects your position in the marketplace*. Recognizing this and building plans to stay on top of the market (to avoid getting dumped into the rapids) are keys to succeeding in sales today.

Other Competitors

Who else competes with you in your marketplace? Do you have many sellers trying to sell their own homes or builders marketing their own properties? These groups can make up a significant percentage of competitors for your commissions. Do market research to find levels and trends of sales activity. You may find new marketing opportunities available from these target markets.

Don't React—Act

Poor planners *react* to competitors' moves in their marketplace. Good planners assess strengths and weaknesses of their competitors and plan *opportunities proactively*. Unfortunately, without good planning processes, many marketers make moves that are only reactions to competitors' moves. Examples of this exist in every field. For years, my husband Dick was a "personality DJ"—one of those gorgeous voices you hear in the morning on the radio, waking you up, making you laugh and revving up the brain cells. To get more listeners during high traffic hours, a rival station created an "auto angel," a person who drove around in a van, announcing traffic conditions and helping stranded motorists. In reaction, Dick's station created their version of an "auto angel"—the "road ranger." Unfortunately, Dick's station became known as a copycat of the first, more innovative station. If his station had regularly held planning sessions and assessed the competition, the station could have made some first moves to gain recognition and higher numbers of listeners.

Up Close and Personal

What does assessing competitors mean to you? Isn't that a company's job? Yes. However, your competition analysis will include both companies and *agents who compete in your world*. You will receive several benefits by conducting your own competition analysis:

1. *You will motivate yourself.* Knowing you have five worthy competitors in your race to list and sell properties, you will subconsciously motivate yourself to refine your programs, sales skills and marketing techniques.

2. *You will be on the cutting edge.* You will be the first to recognize new opportunities, start new programs, take your business to the next highest level.

3. *You will save money.* By integrating company marketing moves into *your personal marketing plan* you will counter both company and agent competitors.

Analyzing the Companies/Offices in Your Area

Figure 2.6 provides the variables to use in analyzing your competition. There are some important points to remember when filling out the grid.

Pick Your Real Competitors. Too often, marketers do not pick their real competitors for their marketplace. They just pick the "big guys," thinking that if they have a dominant market share, every competitor should try to take that market. A good example of this "fuzzy thinking" about competitors came from a new builder. This fellow had been a finish carpenter and planned on building his first four homes that year. He prided himself on his carpentry and his attention to detail. He told me that he would build a better home than the largest builder in our market. What he did not realize was that the largest builder wasn't his competitor because he couldn't compete with some of the benefits a large builder could provide to a customer: a well-planned, large development, a long history of satisfied customers, etc. However, this new builder could compete with other "boutique" builders. If the new builder had known how to pick and assess his *true* competition, he would have been able to create an effective sales story about himself and his product.

Likes Should Compete Against Likes. Your real competitors are the offices that have the market share you think you can take.

Acknowledge Competitors' Strengths. Their strengths are also their weaknesses. A company in our marketplace brags that it is "number one in the area." The company is a local one-office firm; for years it has held a dominant market share in this specific market area. The company communicates that it is the "area expert." And, if that is all the public wanted, this company, unchallenged, could continue to dominate. But what does the public want today? People move in and out of an area—and across the country. Because of the thousands of marketing messages they get daily, confused consumers tend to choose names they recognize. This is not only true in real estate, but in the food industry, clothing industry, in all consumer products and services. Across the nation, companies affiliate with a well-known name for greater market dominance and better services. A smart company in our area would take advantage of the competitor's lack of name recognition outside the area.

☞   What does this mean to you, the agent? In your marketing presentations, you can build a strategy to show your consumer how you and your company fill the consumers' needs. You never mention the weaknesses of the competition, but you do use them in your positive presentation of yourself and your services.

The Statistics: What You're Looking For

All the statistics mentioned are available from your multiple listing service. However, most of the information is not tallied. Gather the data from your computer and tally the results. As you collect your statistics, find the "windows of opportunity." Here are some considerations in each category and suggestions about how to use your findings:

Number of Listings and Number of Sales.   Figure 2.7 shows how you can compare listings or sales by price ranges and companies. Tally the numbers that you are looking for from your multiple listing service; then make a graph. This will show the company's strengths and weaknesses. If the company you are competing against has a greater market share than your company, develop a strategy to exploit the weakness in that dominance. For example, I sold for a large independent real estate company that was number one in the area. Some agents showed the statistics to sellers, saying, "Our company is the largest in the area." The sellers could conclude that they would not get personal service. Now, if you were competing against the largest company, you would create a strategy to exploit their weakness—as your strength.

Listings Taken versus Listings Sold.   If you find that a company takes many listings but sells few, you may want to include that weakness as your strength (if you have better conversion figures). When I started managing my present office, I found that our ratios of listings taken to listings sold was about the same as that of the multiple listing service (about 45 percent). In my former office, our conversion rates were about 85 percent. The best competitor's conversion rates in our area now are about 60 percent. If you were a seller and wanted to get a sold sign on your property, which office would you list with? One of our objectives this year is to increase our conversion ratios to 75 percent. (Next year it will be 85 percent—one step at a time!) Why? In this way we exploit the weakness of the other company

Figure 2.6

Analyzing Your Competition

Best Company Competitors

S = strength W = weakness Names →	S	W	S	W	S	W	S	W	S	W	S	W
Overall marketing strategy												
Competition for listings												
Competition for buyers												
Image/reputation												
Quality of associates												
Rate overall competitive position												

Best Agent Competitors

S = strength W = weakness Names →	S	W	S	W	S	W	S	W	S	W	S	W
Overall marketing strategy												
Competition for listings												
Competition for buyers												
Image reputation												
Quality of associates												
Rate overall competitive position												

as our strength. Our strategy is: We do not list properties to get calls. We list them to get a *sold sign* on the property.

Expired Listings, Time on Market, Price Reductions.   From working in your market, you already know some of your competition's weaknesses. Gather the statistics that support your suppositions, and create a story of strength to take advantage of your competition's weaknesses.

Not the Best Numbers but the Best Strategy.   Recently, I was working with some agents from another office to create a marketing presentation. They were concerned about being able to compete in the market because they did not have the most listings. Guess what? You do not have to be number one to compete successfully. Your success depends on building a sales strategy that exploits the weaknesses you found in your analysis. A few years ago, a very good agent left a dominant number one company to start his own company. He built a story for his new company based on the weaknesses he had found at the dominant number one. His sales strategy was to develop strengths that dominant number one could not replicate. He carefully chose each of his agents—all top producers with builders. He promoted *per agent productivity in that target market*, a promotional statement that the large company could not make. Within a few years, he had built a great "boutique" company that specialized in builders. He took that part of the market share away from dominant number one!

Drawing Conclusions.   A section on the grid in Figure 2.6 will help you draw conclusions about the strengths and weaknesses of the competition. Then you can consider your opportunities in the marketplace. Take time to complete this section. You will find this thought process invaluable as you start to create your marketing plan.

Agents Who Compete with You in Your Marketplace

This point *really* gets up close and personal. If you have worked in your marketplace very long, you find yourself competing against the same agents again and again. It is very frustrating to lose to these particular agents! The grid in Figure 2.6 will help you assess the strengths and weaknesses of your personal competitors. Then you can build a sales strategy to win. Since you work specific markets, relate your competitors to these markets. This is a very important consideration when you consider breaking into a new target market. Let's say you decided to start a geographical market—a *farm*. You picked your area of concentration and made calls. After spending hundreds of hours and hundreds of dollars, you discovered that the farm was "owned" by George. He got 40 percent of all the business in the area; he had worked it for ten years. The residents were

Figure 2.7

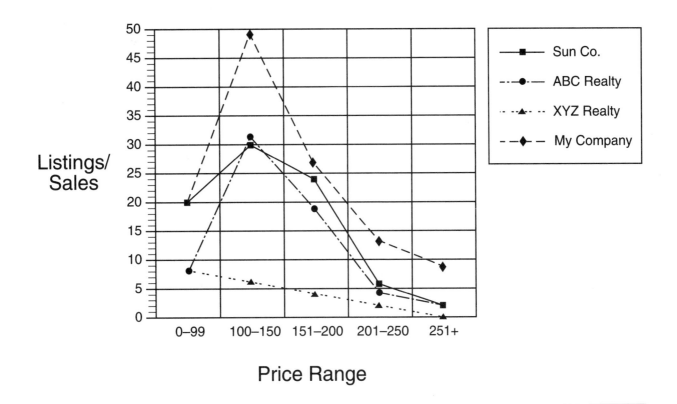

Sales in My Market Area

very loyal to George. If you had done an analysis of the area *before* spending all that time and money, you probably would have decided not to farm this particular area.

Getting Hard-To-Find Information

Gathering statistics about your personal competitors is only part of the analysis process—just as important is finding out exactly *how* they do their business. Why do people like them? How do their listing presentations win listings? How do they work with buyers? What are their strategies in a farm? What is their overall sales strategy? The survey in Figure 2.8 will assist you in gathering this information. Go to buyers and sellers in the target areas where you are competing. Tell consumers that you want to refine your business practices and that you would appreciate their cooperation in answering a few questions. Not only will you get information about your competitors, you will find out what is important to your potential buyers and sellers.

Figure 2.8

Seller Preferences Survey
(phone survey)

Hello. I'm _____ with _____. I'm determining the services that home sellers consider most important in marketing their homes. This survey will take only about four minutes. May I ask you a few questions?

1. How did you determine which agency to list with the last time you sold a home?

   _____ Size
   _____ Reputation
   _____ A friend's recommendation
   _____ Knew the agent
   _____ Approached by the agent
   _____ Ads
   _____ Other _____

2. What services did you consider most effective in selling your home?

   _____

   _____

3. Next time you sell your home, what services will you consider most important.

   _____

   _____

4. What do you look for in a real estate agent?

   _____ Efficiency   _____ Reputation
   _____ Courtesy   _____ Age of firm
   _____ Honesty   _____ Persistence
   _____ Dependability   _____ Knowledge of the market
   _____ Specializes in your area

5. What would you shy away from in a real estate agent?

   _____ Bad attitude   _____ Doesn't make you feel like he or she can
   _____ Pushiness   handle your kind of home
   _____ Part-timer

6. When you list again, will you choose the same agency?

   ____Yes   ____No

   If, yes, because of its: ___ Reputation   ___ Past experience
                           ___ Advertising policies ___ Other

7. Will you list with that particular agent again? ___Yes ___No Why?

8. What services that the agent provided did you find valuable?

   _____

Thank you for your time. Your responses will help me provide better services.

Getting Information When You Win.   Often, when sellers see listing presentations from various companies, they keep the presentations. When you secure a listing, ask to see the competitive presentations. Ask the sellers what they thought was compelling about your presentation. Do the same thing with buyers. As you work with buyers, find out the strategies other agents used in meeting and qualifying them. Ask to see any materials the agents used. By gathering the competition's strategies, you can better refine your sales strategies to become a powerful presenter.

Using Your Company's Analysis To Create Your Plan

Smart companies and offices regularly assess the marketplace, including the competition. Even smarter companies go through this process with their agents and help them to integrate company strategies with specific agent strategies. Knowing your company's analysis and strategy is invaluable as you decide on your marketing moves. As you can imagine, the synergy that results from parallel marketing strategy is awesome.

The easiest way to get this information is to interview your manager. In one of my courses on this planning process, one of the students' assignments is to interview their managers using the form in Figure 2.9. Every student comes back to class with a greater appreciation of the company and a deeper understanding of company marketing strategy. This translates into a better, more powerful agent presentation!

Summary

Looking at the big picture allows you to identify trends. Armed with that information, you can plan strategies and tactics to take advantage of the market—instead of allowing the market to take advantage of you. The next chapter will address your business, providing you the additional information you need to create smart business decisions.

Figure 2.9

Company Analysis/Market Strategy

Overall analysis of the market conditions:

_____

_____

_____

_____

Overall analysis of office position in the market:

Strengths

_____

_____

_____

Challenges

_____

_____

Competitor evaluation:

Main competitors

_____

_____

Strengths

_____

_____

Company/office strategy for the next year:

Markets to capture

_____

_____

Promotional moves planned

_____

Other:

_____

_____

CHAPTER

3

Reviewing Your Business

"Taking time to think about where my business came from and which expenses to discontinue has helped me become more cost-effective."

—Jeanne Castagno

In This Chapter ·

Analyzing your business activities

Identifying your best markets for business

Your business strengths and challenges

Determining levels of customer satisfaction

Your personal internal analysis

You analyzed the larger part of your business environment. Now you need to take a closer look at your business. A review of your personal business will be divided into four sections:

1. A review of your business last year—the statistics, the markets

2. An analysis of your business strengths and challenges

3. An analysis of your customer satisfaction levels

4. A personal internal analysis

These four areas represent all aspects of your business. To be successful, you must keep these areas in balance. Depending on your personality style, you tend to favor certain areas. This can lead to a lopsided business.

Some agents create new business very well but neglect customer service. Then they do not get referrals to help their businesses grow. Dave's business approach provides a good example of imbalance. He came from another sales field where he daily met and closed customers. He tried this approach in real estate. When I was previewing homes one day, I overheard Dave telling a young couple some outrageous information that he made up as he said it. To the first-time buyers, it sounded plausible. Later, when I asked Dave where he had gotten the information, he said that he told the couple what they wanted to hear so that they would buy the home. Dave continued these kinds of business practices. In this particular instance, the couple bought the home and later sued the company and Dave. Needless to say, Dave did not build a good career, even though he made lots of money his first few months in business. If Dave had kept in balance his desire to make money with his desire to provide good customer service, he would still be in business today.

A Review of Your Business Last Year

Figure 3.1 provides the information you need to analyze the amount and types of business you created last year. Let's look at some of the information and draw some conclusions about it to help you make adjustments in your plan for next year. What is your ratio of sales to listings sold? Is that the balance of business that you want? If not, plan the strategies you want to implement to change that balance. You need to create a balance based on your analysis of market trends. If you believe that it will become a buyer's market (many more homes available than buyers), emphasize selling homes in your plan. If you have been a listing specialist and want to continue listing as your specialty in a buyer's market, create some strategies to ensure that your listings sell and that you have a large enough listing inventory to meet your income and profit needs.

Your Ratio of Listings Taken to Listings Sold.   In our multiple listing area, only 45 percent of the total listings sell within any six-month period. What is your personal success ratio? Are you wasting time listing homes that will not sell? If you want to improve your ratio, set a higher goal and create strategies to reach that goal. Then use these high success figures in your personal promotional tactics. Scott, in our office, found that 100 percent of his listings had sold within four days! What a record! So he created postcards to publicize his success record and sent them to areas where he had listing success. He received four phone calls from sending 100 postcards—a very good return on his investment. Success breeds success.

Figure 3.1

A Review of Your Business

Sales _____   Listings taken (LT) _____

Listings sold (LS) _____   % of LT to LS _____

Average time on market for your listings _____ (Break down by price range if desired)

% of sales price to list price for your listings _____   Number of new listings sold _____

Number of resales sold _____   Number of resale listings sold _____

Number of new homes sold _____

Origination of Buyers/Sellers		
	Buyers	Sellers
Reactive Prospecting		
Floor time		
Open houses		
Proactive Prospecting (Segmented by Target Market)		
Past customers/clients		
First-time buyers		
Move-up buyers		
Transferees		
Empty-nesters		
Geographical farm		
Prior business contacts		
Builders		
Other_____		

Of these sellers, which market gave you the most sold listings?

☞   **Keep exploiting these markets. They're your most effective.**

Average Time on the Market for Your Listings. Do you list homes at the right price so that they sell quickly? Or do your listings languish on the market, creating unhappy sellers and poor PR? If you want to shorten your average market time, set some goals and create some strategies to accomplish this.

Your Ratio of Sales Price to List Price. In our multiple listing service, homes sell for 97 percent of last list price. A high ratio of sales price to list price is a very powerful statistic to promote. I saw this strategy in action with a new agent. Nada quickly decided that she would create a career based on high success ratios. She set goals for all the areas above. As she accomplished her goals and measured results, she created very powerful promotions. Since sellers want to work with successful agents, Nada's sales and promotional strategy worked to earn her six figures her first year in real estate. From your analysis of the areas above, you may find that your listing habits have led to long market time, low offers and few listings sold compared to listings taken. Now is the time to create new strategies to change your prior listing results. As you explore the following chapters, you will find ideas for changing these strategies to save time and money—and ensure better results.

Your Business Balance. At the beginning of Chapter 2, I referred to a group of top agents who went through the process you are now completing. After assessing the market trends, they switched their businesses away from new homes to resales and enjoyed much greater success the next year than those who ignored market changes. From breaking down your business into these categories and reflecting on the market trends you previously identified, you will see whether you need to redistribute your business between new homes and resales.

Your Best Markets for Finding Buyers and Sellers Last Year. To determine your best markets, first list all the buyers that you worked with. Make a separate list of all the sellers that you listed. Next identify all the buyers and sellers that you met from holding open houses. Then identify the buyers and sellers that you met from taking floor time. How many buyers and sellers are unidentified? Further in this chapter, we will put these buyers and sellers into groups. But first, let's consider some concepts on generating more business: Where to get leads, and how to get leads.

Open Houses and Floor Time. Sometimes agents find that most of the people who bought and listed with them in the previous year came from open house and floor time contacts. This method of prospecting is termed *reactive*—the agent sits and waits for the customer to come to him or her. Since offices generally schedule agents for these activities, agents may consider that carrying out these scheduled activities is actually the "business plan." However, I found, from completing agent surveys, that agents who rely on open houses and floor time for leads make average incomes—at best. If these activities guaranteed each agent's income goals, every agent going into the business would make lots of money—and stay in the business. And every agent in the business would realize his income goals. Unfortunately, neither is true. Each year over half the agents in real estate are new. One reason for this is that agents find it easier to sit and wait for customers to come to them than to go out and contact potential customers and clients. Also agents believe that office scheduling will guarantee them the number and quality of contacts they need to reach their goals. In the '90s relying on reactive contact methods to deliver the leads you need to assure your goals is a sure way to go broke! Today's public is more discerning and less liable to rely on a stranger. People choose agents based on referrals; they interview agents to determine the best agent for their needs. In addition, more agents aggressively seek new customers and clients.

Successful agents go out into the field, meet people and convert them to customers and clients *before* the potential customer or client makes the effort to pick up the phone or go to an open house. Trends of the '90s include: more aggressive agent prospecting, more discerning customers/clients, less effective floor time and open houses.

Should You Drop Open Houses and Floor Time? It depends on your market. Let's go back to that valuable market analysis section. What kind of market would encourage buyers to come into open houses in great numbers, or to call your office? A seller's market. So, if you are in a market with many buyers who, because of market conditions, are afraid to wait to purchase, schedule more open houses (if you like that strategy to find buyers and sellers). To be sure that you get enough leads, you should do two things:

1. Contact homeowners in the area to invite them to the open house and ask for leads. This increases the number of potential contacts you will have from this activity, and it provides you PR as a successful real estate salesperson.

2. Increase your sales skill in open houses by taking a workshop to practice meeting, greeting, qualifying and closing contacts for appointments. If you want to rely on floor time to deliver some of your leads, increase your sales skill to take advantage of those who

call you. In addition, support your office's operations by cooperating with its schedule. See your manager to help you get a balance of your time allotted to various prospecting methods.

Switching Your Emphasis to Proactive Methods.   The opposite of reactive prospecting methods is *proactive* techniques. That means that the agent actively goes out to contact potential buyers and sellers. This method is the one that all good salespeople emphasize—because they want to ensure their incomes. You cannot *make* people come to your open houses. But you can be assured of 50 leads in a certain period of time if you knock on doors in a particular area. What are proactive methods? Phone calls and in-person calls. But who do you call on? To answer that question, let's go back to the unidentified sellers and buyers you listed earlier. Do you have few or none in the unidentified category? That means, to increase your business next year, you should switch much of your emphasis from reactive to proactive contact methods.

Connecting the Proactive Idea to Marketing Concepts.   Okay, you are convinced. You will proactively contact many people next year to get leads. But who are these people, and where are you going to find them? To answer that question, let's use a marketing concept. Marketers have found that contacting everyone who might ever buy anything is not an efficient or effective way to market their products and services. In fact, with today's huge diverse populations, it is not even possible. Because consumers are "overcommunicated with," they often do not pay attention when someone contacts them about something they are not interested in. Look at your mail for the next few days. Can you figure out *why* you received those particular sales pieces? They relate to your life habits, your interests, your inquiries. Marketers have information about you or from you to indicate that you, at some time in your life, would be interested in what they have to sell. This marketing concept—marketing to specific groups who marketers determined are real potential buyers for their particular products or services— is called *target marketing*. You can apply these proven marketing principles to your problem of figuring out *who* to call on.

Segmenting Your Buyers and Sellers.   Do you remember the buyers and sellers that you did not meet from open houses and/or from floor time? These buyers and sellers can be segmented into identifiable groups. Marketers segment by using *demographics*—statistics and psychographics—life habits. By grouping people, you create *target markets*. Knowing that these targeted people have common needs and interests,

Figure 3.2

Which "Career" Do You Want?

The following are descriptions of the kind and number of activities agents do to create certain levels of business. These are taken from studies of particular agents' daily schedules and their results.

A Reactive-Based Plan   *½ transaction per month**

To generate business: Reactive activities only
Leads from floor time and open house

A Blended Plan   *1½ transactions per month*

To generate business: ½ reactive / ½ proactive activities
Reactive leads from floor time and open house = ½ transaction
Proactive leads from 100 contacts/mo. = 1 transaction

A Proactive-Based Plan   *2+ transactions per month*

To generate business: ¼ reactive / ¾ proactive
Reactive leads from floor time and open house = ½ transaction
Proactive leads from 200 contacts/mo. = 2 transactions

---

*This is 2 transactions/year higher than the average in a large multiple listing service with over 9,000 members.

you can create promotional tactics in your marketing plan that speak to and appeal to each of these groups. Target markets could include:

- First-time buyers
- Empty nesters
- Geographical farms
- Past customers/clients
- Move-up buyers
- Social groups
- Business contacts
- Builders

Start thinking of these groups as your potential targets for *future* business. Prioritize them by the amount of business they gave you last year. Which were your best sources? You can create an even more dynamic marketing plan to get more business from them next year. In the discussion on marketing (see Chapter 8), I will show you a simple yet effective method to create promotions that will yield results from your best target markets.

Balancing Proactive versus Reactive.   From your analysis, if you found you got more than one-quarter of your leads from reactive methods, emphasize *proactive* methods next year (see Figure 3.2).

In the '90s, you must create an aggressive, dynamic self-run business plan to compete with agents, serve demanding consumer needs and realize your income goals. Figure 3.2 shows the results of working a reactive-based plan or a proactive-based plan. Notice as the agent switches to a proactive-based plan, the results increase.

Your Business Strengths and Challenges

Using Figure 3.3, analyze your business strengths and challenges. This analysis works in tandem with the analysis you just completed. As you work through this chapter, think of ways to improve or refine your business skills. You will see patterns of excellence and patterns of challenge. Generally, when agents are good at finding buyers, they are good at finding sellers. It is common, too, that low productivity results from an *imbalance* of ratings. For example, Joan considered herself good at promoting the properties she had listed, but her ratio of listings taken to listings sold was low. She also rated herself low on prospecting for new listings.

After thinking through these evaluations, Joan decided that she could increase her productivity by prospecting for better qualified listings. Then

Figure 3.3

Analysis: Your Business Strengths and Challenges

Rate yourself as: 1 = Excellent   2 = Very Good

3 = Fair   4 = Needs Improvment

Activity	Rating
Sales	
Finding potential buyers (proactive)	
Evaluating buying potential	
Following up with potential buyers	
Interviewing, qualifying buyers, building rapport	
Showing properties buyers want to see	
Helping buyers make buying decisions—closing	
Evaluating time spent in helping each buyer (too much, not enough?)	

Activity	Rating
Listing	
Finding potential sellers (proactive)	
Qualifying sellers	
Evaluating marketability of product	
Giving an effective listing presentation	
Closing for a listing	
Promoting property	
Time on market for my properties	

Activity	Rating
Skills/Operations	
Counseling skills with buyers	
Negotiating the earnest money agreement	
Follow-up prior to closing	
Follow-up after closing—building referral business	
Distribution plan for marketing myself	
Telephone skills	
Open house skills	

her properties would sell more often and faster, and she would have to spend less time and money on promotions. After completing this page, use this analysis to set goals for yourself in the professional development section of the business plan.

Determining Your Levels of Customer Satisfaction

Experienced agents know that the key to building a dynamic real estate business is to *create referral business*. How do you convince your previous customers and clients to come back to you? How do you convince them to provide you with new leads?

Besides creating a marketing plan to this target market (see Chapter 6) a key is to *provide excellent customer service.*

How do you know that you are providing what the customer wants—at a high level of customer service? I ask agents that question when I am teaching business planning. Many agents tell me that they know the customer was happy with the service "when the customer who bought from them lists with them when they're ready to sell." However, since that time frame is anywhere from 1 to 20 years, it is also possible that a customer could be unhappy all that time. But the agent would never know it until the customer was ready to sell and did not list with the agent! There are many dangers in not knowing your levels of customer satisfaction. According to consumer research, the unhappy customer *doesn't* generally complain; he just does not come back. That is not the end of the story, however. According to consumer surveys and common sense, *the unhappy customer tells nine people!* When people go to a restaurant that provides poor service, their natural inclination is not to complain to management. Generally, they handle the situation by never going back to the restaurant. In addition, people tend to share their discontent to potential restaurant clientele—clever the way we get back at the restaurant for poor customer service, isn't it? Less-than-thrilled real estate customers and clients act the same way, costing hundreds of missed opportunities to create more business from prior business. However, if you developed a *cycle of customer satisfaction*, you could dramatically increase your business. You *can* create this cycle. It starts with finding out how you are doing. Market research will provide those answers. Using the survey provided in Figure 3.4, you can find out your customer levels of satisfaction. After you have determined your areas of strength and needed improvements, write these into your plan on professional development (see Chapter 9).

In addition to the survey for your customers and clients, I have provided a survey for *you* to complete (see Figure 3.5). This survey compares the

Figure 3.4

Customer Survey

Dear _____ ,
Congratulations on the closing of your home. I'm happy that I could help you. So that I can evaluate and refine my service, I would appreciate your comments and suggestions. Your opinion is important to me. Please help me by returning this form in the self-addressed, stamped envelope at your earliest convenience. Your comments will ensure that I am providing the highest level services available! Thank you.

Specifically, how would you rate me on these items?

1. Source of information   ___ Excellent ___ Satisfactory ___ Unsatisfactory

2. Keeping you informed   ___ Excellent ___ Satisfactory ___ Unsatisfactory

3. Problem solving   ___ Excellent ___ Satisfactory ___ Unsatisfactory

4. Listening skills   ___ Excellent ___ Satisfactory ___ Unsatisfactory

5. Availability   ___ Excellent ___ Satisfactory ___ Unsatisfactory

6. Enthusiasm   ___ Excellent ___ Satisfactory ___ Unsatisfactory

7. Easy to work with   ___ Excellent ___ Satisfactory ___ Unsatisfactory

What did you like about working with me? _____

_____

Would you recommend me to others? ___ Yes ___ No

May I use you as a reference? ___ Yes ___ No

What areas could I improve on? _____

Services you would like to see me add: _____

_____

Would you refer your friends and family to me? _____

How would you like me to continue communication? _____

Would you write a letter of recommendation for me? _____

Who do you know who's interested in buying or selling in the future? _____

Names and phone numbers: _____

_____

Signature:_____ Date: _____

services *you* provide with the services thousands of buyers and sellers said they wanted from real estate agents. I created this evaluation from the comments of thousands of buyers and sellers interviewed by Consumer Reports in 1991. Without knowing the level of consumer demand, it is easy to assume that you provide customer service that meets your consumers' needs. In other words, because the consumer did not take action and complain, you provided wonderful levels of customer service. In reality, you may be missing the mark.

Finding Out Where You Stand Can Be Shocking.   Why don't agents and real estate companies regularly survey their customers and clients? Perhaps they do not realize the value. Maybe it is too much trouble. Or perhaps *agents are afraid to find out*. But let's look at the rest of the story. According to consumers (that's us, in real life, by the way), if the product/ service provider quickly discovers that customers are dissatisfied and *fixes it fast*, over 90 percent of them will come back again! Actually, many times consumers simply want someone to *listen* to their complaint.

Just think what could happen to the image of the real estate industry if a system to drive a cycle of customer satisfaction were created (see Figure 3.6). For more information on how to measure and provide high levels of customer satisfaction to enhance your business results, see the list of books provided in the Reference section.

Personal Internal Analysis

When you entered the real estate business, you no doubt heard that real estate salespeople needed to be *self-starters*. As you can tell from your own real estate experience, that's more than true! No amount of analysis and planning will ensure a successful real estate career. Only implementing the plan ensures success. But the best-laid plans oft go awry because we have not emotionally bought into the plan. Challenges and barriers in our lives get in the way of accomplishing our goals. Using the analytical tools in this chapter, look at these considerations and start developing ways to motivate yourself past these challenges and barriers. Prepare for setting goals for yourself in your professional development. Jot down ideas to handle the personal challenges that will arise, such as who will fix dinner when you're at a listing presentation.

Sometimes the fear of success is greater than the fear of failure. People dread changing their lives to coordinate the added stresses, demands and even rewards of increased business. By completing this personal internal analysis (see Figure 3.7), you will be thinking ahead, creating a better

Figure 3.5

Establishing Trust:
Creating a High Level of Customer Satisfaction

	ALWAYS	SOMETIMES	NEVER
For sellers:			
Create a marketing plan in writing for their home.	☐	☐	☐
Explain your marketing plan in writing.	☐	☐	☐
Tell sellers before you do a promotion.	☐	☐	☐
Promptly send sellers copy of promotion.	☐	☐	☐
Promptly tell sellers results of promotion.	☐	☐	☐
Have a listing presentation book, and show it to all sellers.	☐	☐	☐
Have list of satisfied sellers, and give to seller.	☐	☐	☐
Explain your market analysis.	☐	☐	☐
Present market analysis in writing.	☐	☐	☐
Review market analysis with sellers at least monthly.	☐	☐	☐
Turn down a listing if it's overpriced. (You value your integrity more than you are tempted to put your sign in the yard to get calls.)	☐	☐	☐
For buyers:			
Qualify by using a questionnaire, and write the answers.	☐	☐	☐
Show homes *after* you have qualified buyers in all aspects.	☐	☐	☐
Ask the qualifying question: How will you use this?	☐	☐	☐
Preview homes before showing.	☐	☐	☐
Level with buyers if homes don't exist in their price range.	☐	☐	☐
Refer them to another agent if you don't know the neighborhood.	☐	☐	☐
Check the services, amenities, schools, etc. of the neighborhood, and keep the information current.	☐	☐	☐
When qualifying, match timeframes and expectations.	☐	☐	☐
Listen two-thirds of the time. Talk one-third of the time when you're with them. Write down their answers and review.	☐	☐	☐
Tell them the defects you note in the property.	☐	☐	☐
Tell them the bad news first.	☐	☐	☐
Explain how "agency" works.	☐	☐	☐
Gracefully withdraw offers.	☐	☐	☐
Create referral business from those you didn't "sell."	☐	☐	☐

These are the services perceived as valuable to clients and customers. When you consistently provide these services, you create high levels of customer satisfaction, loyalty and referral business.

Figure 3.6

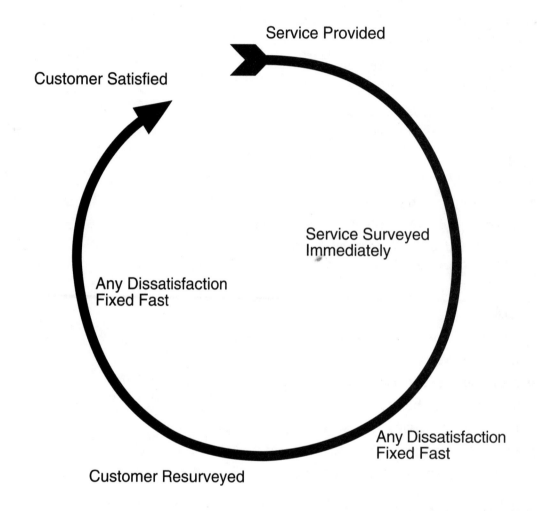

Customer Satisfaction Cycle

Service Provided

Customer Satisfied

Service Surveyed
Immediately

Any Dissatisfaction
Fixed Fast

Any Dissatisfaction
Fixed Fast

Customer Resurveyed

movie for yourself as a great real estate pro—and enjoying your family and interests while having a wonderful career.

Good Results Can Change Bad Attitude. Which comes first? A good attitude, from which good business practices result, or good business practices, which create success, which create good attitude? Psychologists have argued endlessly about whether attitude determines results or whether results determine attitude. Many agents look to motivational seminars, tapes and talks to "pump them up" and change their attitudes about aspects

Figure 3.7

Personal Internal Analysis

Analysis of your attitude toward your business:

_____

_____

_____

Barriers that deterred you from attaining your business goals last year:

_____

_____

_____

Personal challenges—family:

_____

_____

_____

Possible solutions:

_____

_____

_____

Personal challenges—other:

_____

_____

_____

Possible solutions:

_____

_____

_____

Recognized motivators in my past:

_____

_____

_____

How I can motivate myself to address the barriers and challenges above:

_____

_____

_____

of the real estate business. They think they must have the right attitude to take certain actions. However, from practicing and performing music, I discovered that you can change your attitude about something by just doing it. That is, accept a bad attitude about something, and go ahead and try it. After you have successfully completed the activity, *your success changes your attitude about the activity*! For example, Joanne, in our office, had never "cold called"—that is, picked up the phone and called strangers to ask for leads. She had a bad attitude about cold calling. However, she desperately wanted to make money and meet the performance standards required to remain affiliated with our office. So she tried cold calling. As predicted, Joanne hated cold calling at first. But, after she improved her technique (through practice), she got results. Joanne began to like cold calling, and now she *loves* it because it brings results.

☞ The bottom line is: If you have been looking for short-term motivators to get your business going, quit. Just start doing things; you will achieve success. *Success* is the biggest, best motivator. Examine your own attitude as you complete this section of planning. Identify barriers to your success, personal challenges, areas you want to work on. Then establish a plan to get to work. Adopt the Nike motto: *Just do it.*

Summary

To many impatient, action-oriented agents, this chapter on getting ready may seem to get in your way. You are anxious to get to the good part—the creative, innovative, attention-getting action steps. However, not knowing what you are getting into, spending your money unwisely and wasting time are the consequences of skipping this first step in the planning process. And I am sure that all agents would agree that time and resource management are our greatest challenges.

Gathering the information explained in this chapter has many benefits. It will guide you in the general direction to take your business. You can put your research to work in your personal promotion and in sellers' marketing plans. After you have gathered this information once, you merely have to update your information, testing assumptions and comparing trends to get a handle on the future of your real estate career. With real estate practices changing so rapidly, the need for immediate trend identification and change has never been greater. As the '90s progress, you will see more agents becoming savvy researchers—capable and armed for making good, informed business decisions.

CHAPTER

Capturing Your Focus

"Use your mission statement in promotions. This whole system has helped me break my plan into 'chewable bites.' "

—Sue Bates-Pintar

In This Chapter ·

The importance of focus

Vision statements

Creating your vision

The Importance of Focus

You analyzed your business. You narrowed your fields to those target markets that bring you the best business and with whom you feel most comfortable. Now you are ready to capture a snapshot of you, the businessperson—a photo in perfect focus. That's easy: You already have that snapshot—you are a real estate salesperson. Well, so are 1,500,000 other licensees—and that is just in the United States! To attract the kind of customers and clients you want, you need to create a more focused picture—one that communicates your special talents, markets and services. Otherwise, how could a customer choose you from all the other real estate licensees in your area?

Think of restaurants. How long has it been since you drove past restaurant row and saw a sign that read "food"? Today, communicating a message is much more challenging than in the past. Consumers get an estimated 500,000 marketing messages a year, each of which asks them to *pay attention*. However, people do not pay attention to all these messages; they select those that seem to speak directly to them. When you are in a crowd, where everyone is talking, you do not pay attention *until your name is called*. You are selectively paying attention to messages. Marketers have discovered that, to attract anyone to their products or services, they must stop being generalists, e.g., food. Instead, they must narrow their focus to a type of food, e.g., Italian food.

Does narrowing your focus restrict your number of customers? Sure. But, if a food sign brings in no one and an Italian food sign brings in enough customers for the restaurant to thrive, which is the right marketing move?

In addition, refining your focus will help you choose the activities that build your career, rather than merely engaging in any real estate activities. When I was a new agent, I sold a home to friends on an island 30 miles from where I lived and worked. Since they were friends, I thought that it would be okay to sell them the home, rather than refer them to an agent on the island. So we ventured off to find the island and the house. How did my friends view my professional image? Was my confidence rising or ebbing? I found the home, but I could not tell my customers anything about the area, waterfront, land, etc.—confidence was diminishing. I did sell my friends the home. However, the time spent and the difficulty of the sale must have earned me about $1.25 an hour for my efforts!

If you are a relatively new agent, you might think that collecting a commission is your *most important objective*. However, for any agent, *making the career moves that build a career are the most important objectives*. And you will make more money faster! While I concentrated on selling the home on the island, I lost:

- the time to prospect for customers and clients *in my area of expertise*—the area where I needed to build my image.

- the focus I needed to communicate with the potential customers and clients who would refer others to me *in my area of expertise*.

- the education and confidence I needed to build *in my area of expertise* to serve my desired customers and clients.

- the ability to promote myself based on that sale. This is an important point. Agents can only market themselves on our *successes*. For me to knock on doors on that island to tell them I was the agent who sold that home would not have made sense. By pursuing one commission, I lost ten commissions!

I did not consider the consumer in this scenario. Because I did not know the market area, I put both the seller and the buyer at a disadvantage. From this experience, I learned to *narrow my focus*. I learned that I could not be merely a licensee and provide good service to customers and clients or build a career.

Vision Statements

You can capture your focus by going through a process that results in what companies call vision or mission statements. These, *statements of purpose*, communicate:

- the specific business you are in;
- the geographical target markets you serve;
- the services you provide;
- the specific groups of people you provide service to; and
- your business ideals.

If I had created that statement at the beginning of my career, I would have benefited in several ways. I could have:

- made better decisions about where to spend my time and dollars;
- better served my customers and clients; and
- more effectively promoted myself.

 Completing statements of purpose is an agent's *most important thought process* in order to create a dynamic, professional career—quickly. An agent's biggest challenge is time management. If you do not create business guidelines *before* you take action, you will jump from one activity to another—building an activity maze, rather than a recognizable career picture.

As You Capture Your Focus

From working with hundreds of real estate agents and companies in crafting statements of purpose, I have discovered some areas to watch for as you craft your vision statement:

It Must Have a Well-Defined Focus. You should be able to give this statement to a stranger and expect it to provide a clear picture of you and your business. This is what a well-defined focus will do for you: Imagine that a stranger is driving past thousands of real estate agents—all with neon signs flashing "licensee" in neon flashing around their necks. However, your sign flashes "specialist in . . . ." The stranger stops and selects you— because you stood out from all the "generic" salespeople. All consumers must differentiate before choosing a particular product or service. You want your public to differentiate you from all other real estate salespeople. Then you can work toward standing out from all others in your field. As a result, you create an image as the customer's *agent of choice*. In marketing, this is called *positioning*. That means that a product or service occupies the position of choice in the consumer's mind.

Although Kleenex® is a brand name, the manufacturer has done such a good job of positioning in the consumer's mind that Kleenex® has become a generic term for all tissues! Wouldn't it be wonderful if, when your target markets thought of real estate, your name popped into their minds? Completing the thought process and writing your vision statement is the first step to assuring that you are positioned in your target market's mind as the real estate expert of choice.

It Must Be Restrictive.   We simply cannot be all things to all people. Besides, in today's marketing world, that approach no longer works. Look at your analysis of your business. Drop the activities that have not brought success, and focus on those that have been successful. After all, you are much more than a licensee. But to communicate that idea, you must repeat the same activities again and again until your desired public gets the message. Scattering your efforts will not provide the consistent repetition needed to establish an image with your desired markets.

Look at the kinds of business you have been doing. Are you dabbling in commercial real estate, while residential real estate brings you most of your business? Is your consumer best served by your dabbling? Are you wasting your precious resources of time and money educating yourself in an area where you get little return? Drop the businesses that give you little return. Instead, establish referral bases with commercial specialists—and get residential referrals from them. All real estate salespeople would make more money by establishing referral networks and letting specialists help consumers. In fact, the licensee who does not refer to other specialists will experience a declining income.

It Must Complement Your Office and Company Visions.   Although this seems to be a commonsense concept, it is difficult to actualize. The first office I managed specialized in residential real estate. The office had no commercial division and no support services for commercial real estate: no commercial training, no commercial multiple listing service membership, no advertising budget for commercial properties. The public knew our company as a *residential specialist*. One day a fellow came to my office for an interview; he wanted to list apartment buildings. He said he could bring in lots of commissions. The money sounded great. What harm could it be to add one more agent, doing business a little differently? So I hired him. Then the "harm" started. The agent advertised his apartments. When the other agents (residential specialists) received calls about these apartments, they had no idea of what to say to the callers. The commercial agent asked the agents to refer all the calls to him; the residential agents replied that they did not consider themselves to be his secretaries!

Stepping out of your specialty, whether you are an office or an agent, is not good for your business health. If you want to open a commercial division, create a plan with all the support services you need to become a *competent specialist*. Today, any other attitude will only cost time and money. As you name your specialties, ask yourself: Do I have all the support services I need to professionally serve my consumer in this specialty? Can I compete with other agents and agencies in this specialty? If you cannot answer yes to both questions, either drop the specialty or open your own specialty division.

Some Fine Points

Because focus statements are really statements of you as a businessperson, these statements are not lightly changed—just as you would not lightly change *yourself*. That does not mean that you might not work over time on how your statement is constructed, but it does mean that you do not change the essence of the statement, the specialties, the ideals— without considerable thought.

Statements should be written in the *present tense*. These statements convey you at your best—how you see yourself as a real estate professional. Because you may not have actually attained the picture you have in mind, you may be writing about yourself as *you see yourself in the future*. To cement that thought in your mind, use present tense verbs as you create your statement. Read how differently these statements below communicate this agent's picture of success:

- I will become a successful agent. (Future Tense)
- I am a successful agent. (Present Tense)

Using present tense verbs leads you to become the agent you desire. For, as the truism states: "As you think, so you become."

Figure 4.1

Tips on Vision Statements

Vision statements should be:
- Well-defined
- Restrictive
- Complementary with your company statement

Vision statements are:
- Not lightly changed
- Written in the present tense
- Not objectives
- Not tied to time

Vision statements include:
- Statement of what you specialize in
- Where you work
- Areas you serve
- Your target markets (people)
- Your values
- Your services

Vision Statements Are Not Objectives

Vision statements are not quantifiable. Leave out any numbers—they go into your objectives. Following is an example: A person may write, "I am a profitable agent. I will make a profit of $50,000 every year." The first part of the statement, "I am a profitable agent" has a place in a mission statement. But the last part of the statement is an objective, or quantifiable end result, and should be placed in another section of your plan. The vision statement is broader; it guides you as you make long-term decisions. Figure 4.1 offers some valuable tips on writing vision statements.

Examples of Vision Statements

Figure 4.2 provides several examples of agents' mission statements. Note how different they are. Without ever meeting these agents, you could probably choose the one you would feel most comfortable with, the one who would serve the specialty markets that appeal to you.

Figure 4.3 is a worksheet for creating the portions of your mission statement. Take the time to complete this worksheet. You will reap the benefits of this process as you create all parts of your business plan.

Summary

One of the keys to your success is to think of yourself as a company. One reason companies fail is that they have no clear idea of who they are. They try to be all things to all people. Just as a company must narrow its focus to succeed, so must you. In doing so, you will be able to communicate with the people who want your services. This means leaving out some potential clienteles. But by providing a precise focus to your activities, you will quickly build a strong career, save yourself marketing dollars and provide the levels of customer service that your consumers expect.

Because vision statements represent your values and ideals, you will get inspiration from writing and reading your vision statement. This inspiration is invaluable as you tackle the everyday challenges in your real estate career.

Figure 4.2

Agents' Personal Visions

"I am a residential REALTOR®, specializing in the listing and sale of new and resale residential properties on the east side of Lake Washington. I create long-term business relationships with my clients and customers through exceptional services; I want to be known as their "REALTOR® for life." In order to provide this level of service, I constantly update my real estate information and skills."

"I am a successful REALTOR® with ABC Realty, which specializes in residential home and land sales. My business consists of working with both buyers and sellers. My customers include first-time and move-up buyers, retirees, builders and developers. My clients, in turn, are builders, developers and sellers who use my professional services to market the sale of their property. I take pride in my job by demonstrating a professional attitude with my buyers and sellers. My customers and clients value me because of my follow-through efforts; they appreciate my sincerity, honesty and sense of humor in dealing with them. I am successful because I provide to my customers and clients products and services that others are unable or unwilling to provide."

- I am a real estate professional.
- I specialize in residential properties.
- My clients and customers are upwardly mobile and established professionals.
- My premise of service is to find out what people want and help them get it.
- I proceed with honest, intelligent effort.
- I bring to my clients a sincere concern for their welfare.

Figure 4.3

Creating Your Vision

What you do: _____
_____
_____
_____

Where you sell: _____
_____
_____
_____

What you sell (properties): _____
_____
_____
_____

What you specialize in (your target properties, buyers, sellers): _____
_____
_____
_____

What you don't/won't sell—geographical types of sellers, buyers, properties, other kinds
of real estate (this is to help you refine your focus; it is not for publication): _____
_____
_____

Your business values: _____
_____
_____

Talents, specialties, competencies you bring from your other fields: _____
_____
_____

Benefits: _____
_____
_____
_____

How you are different from other real estate people: _____
_____
_____
_____

CHAPTER

5

Setting Your Objectives

"I have really benefited from setting objectives so that I can be sure I'm spending time on projects that return profits."

—Lorna Willard

In This Chapter ·

Real estate and your life

Determining your desired results

What's measured and why

Measuring your results for self-management

Starting at the End

Your vision statement helped you define your focus so that you could see yourself as the *epitome of your definition of success*. To accomplish that, you projected your mind into the future and created a strong "mind picture" of yourself as a career pro. In this chapter, you will look at the end in a different way—by defining the results you want from your business. These results, or objectives, can be one-year, three-year or even five-year projections. Some agents even project ten or twenty years. As you delve into the world of objectives, you will see that the process of creating objectives in business or your personal life is exactly the same. In each case, you decide exactly where you want to be at the end of your journey. Then you plot the path to get there.

Real Estate and Your Life

Having been a real estate practitioner for two decades, I realize that real estate is truly a way of life—business associates become friends, friends become customers, family becomes integrated into career. It's difficult to determine where real estate leaves off and private life starts. As I pondered this chapter, I decided to address the obvious first. Real estate results have no meaning in our lives unless they are integrated into our life goals. You should make a few decisions in your life's "big picture" *before* you tackle your specific real estate goals. Figure 5.1 provides an internal analysis for looking at potential life goals. There are also many good books and programs on life goal-setting. Take the time to think through these questions before you create your one-year real estate objectives.

There's more to life than money. In fact, in my experience, agents who told me that they "wanted to make a lot of money" frequently *made little money* in real estate. The reason was that they did not know what the money was *for*. Jeannette had been an agent for ten years. In the prior year, she had made $40,000. But the next year she had made only $3,000 by July! Why? The market changed, but Jeannette refused to change her sales strategies to match the new market. I asked her how much money she wanted to make that year. She told me she wanted to make $50,000. Knowing that she lived on a modest income, I asked her what she wanted to do with the money. She said she hadn't thought about it, but was sure that making a lot of money was important. However, by the end of that year, she had made only $6,000. By her behavior, Jeannette proved that making a lot of money really wasn't as important to her as maintaining the business practices that had worked for her in the past. In other words, Jeannette needed to *change* in order to realize her monetary goals. Change was more difficult than her need for money was motivating.

What Are Your Life Priorities?

Too often, I have seen agents' other life priorities interfere with their objectives in real estate. Recognize your life priorities *first*. Otherwise, you may set up real estate objectives that are unattainable at that point in your life. Jeannie, in my office, told me that she wanted to make $50,000 in the coming year in real estate. She had made that amount two years ago but had experienced health and relationship problems the next year. Her income had dropped to $18,000. She set her goal for $50,000 and completed her plan. As I read her plan, I realized that she would not reach her $50,000 goal. She had written repeatedly: I'll do research to determine if . . .; I'll decide if I want to . . .; I'll see if there is something I want to do . . . . These were all variations of the same theme—*getting ready to get ready*. Jeannie

Figure 5.1

Life Goals

You are now retired. Describe your ideal life: _____
_____
_____
_____

You are retired looking back over your life. Your comments: _____
_____
_____
_____

You are listening in as friends, business associates, customers and clients discuss you. What are they saying? _____
_____
_____
_____

What do you want to be when you grow up? _____
_____
_____
_____

How can real estate assure you of becoming that person? _____
_____
_____

You have $5 million. How will you spend it? _____
_____
_____

Figure 5.2

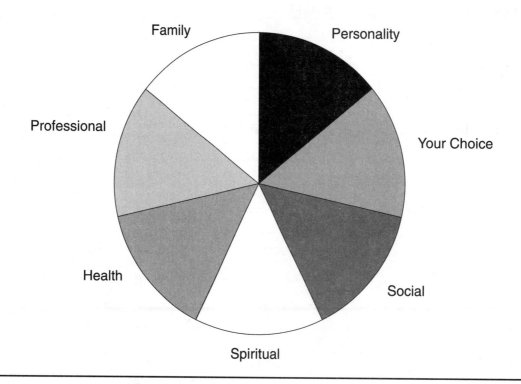

Life Balance

still had barriers in the rest of her life—barriers that had to be removed before she could double her real estate income. I met with Jeannie, and we talked about the language of the plan and what it meant. She was indecisive about the next year. Finally, she decided to take a leave of absence to concentrate on her current priorities. I appreciated Jeannie's honesty and encouraged her to take care of her priorities. Do you have barriers in your life that must be removed before you can reach your real estate objectives? Take advantage of your office's support systems to recognize and remove those barriers—your manager, training programs and perhaps counseling. Figure 5.2 illustrates the balance needed between goals to maintain a *life balance*.

Creating Real Estate Objectives

You have put real estate into your big picture. Now, it's time to bring the focus closer to your real estate objectives. This book will guide you as you establish objectives in two real estate areas:

1. *Expanding your business* (includes marketing). This is where you set monetary and activity objectives. These measurable objectives guide you daily as you complete the specific activities that help you to expand your business. In addition, you will set some overall sales strategy objectives that will help you to be more effective and efficient in your business.

2. *Professional development.* These objectives help you *support* your business: education, organization, research, staff, etc.

Determining Your Desired Results

In creating your objectives, the first step is to create your budget. You should consider three budget areas. These are expenses that *must* be covered for you to run your business. The total expenses of these three areas create your *budget*:

1. *Personal operating expenses.* How much money do you need to live? Figure 5.3 is a worksheet for figuring out what you need to "take home" to pay your bills.

2. *Real estate operating expenses.* These are the expenses you accrue in your daily business activities. Figure 5.4 divides these expenses into categories to help you project these expenses.

3. *Marketing expenses.* These expenses (or investments), which you make to promote your business (personal marketing, support staff, etc.) should make up 10 to 20 percent of your gross income. For now, simply estimate the total amount of expenses you will dedicate to marketing. To get a sense of your total budget, put that estimated figure at the top of the worksheet in Figure 5.4. (You will assign budget amounts to each target market and tally those amounts in Figure 8.13 in Chapter 8.) Refine your real estate budget and objectives to reflect these costs. The total of the three areas creates your needed income and forms your total budget.

That's Not All There Is to Life

Since real estate is an integral part of your life, let's add the fun. What's all that work for, anyhow? Where do you want to go? What do you want to do? What fun do you want to have next year? What do you want to do for your loved ones? Put a monetary figure in this category, then put these numbers into Figure 5.5 to show the *amount of money you want to make next year to cover your expenses and dreams.*

Figure 5.3

Personal Operating Expenses

Regular Monthly Payments

House payments (principal, interest, taxes, insurance, condominium fees or rent) • • • $ _____

Car payments (including insurance) • $ _____

Appliance, TV payments • $ _____

Home improvement loan payments • $ _____

Personal loan, credit card payments • $ _____

Health plan payments • $ _____

Life insurance payments • $ _____

Other insurance payments • $ _____

Total • $ _____

Household Operating Expenses

Telephone • $ _____

Gas and electricity • $ _____

Water • $ _____

Other household expenses, repairs, maintenance • • • • • • • • • • • • • • • • • • • $ _____

Total • $ _____

Personal Expenses

Clothing, cleaning, laundry • $ _____

Prescription medications • $ _____

Physicians, dentists • $ _____

Education • $ _____

Dues • $ _____

Gifts and contributions • $ _____

Newspapers, magazines, books • $ _____

Auto upkeep and gas (part may go in your real estate budget) • • • • • • • • • • • • $ _____

Children's school tuition • $ _____

Spending money and allowances • $ _____

Miscellaneous • $ _____

Total • $ _____

Food Expenses

Food—at home • $ _____

Food—away from home • $ _____

Total • $ _____

Tax Expenses

Federal and state income taxes • $ _____

Other taxes not included above • $ _____

Total • $ _____

Total Personal Monthly Expenses • $ _____

Total Personal Yearly Expenses • $ [_____]

Figure 5.4

Your Real Estate Budget
Real Estate Operating Expenses

	Yearly	Monthly
Total marketing budget	$ _____	$ _____
Professional fees (REALTORS®, MLS)	$ _____	$ _____
Business car expenses (gas, oil, tools, repair)	$ _____	$ _____
Communications expenses (pager, phone)	$ _____	$ _____
Labor/mechanical (from systems worksheet)	$ _____	$ _____
Professional development (from worksheet)	$ _____	$ _____
Supplies	$ _____	$ _____
Business insurance	$ _____	$ _____
Legal fees	$ _____	$ _____
Licenses, permits	$ _____	$ _____
Other	$ _____	$ _____
Total	$ _____	$ _____

Add the Profit

There's one more category in Figure 5.5—*profit*. Just covering your expenses isn't nearly as much fun as making a profit. What profit do you want to make? Add that number to Figure 5.5. Now the total figure is the amount of money that you want to make next year to cover your expenses, realize your dreams and make a profit. The pie chart in Figure 5.6 illustrates a total real estate operating budget.

Figure 5.5

Deciding the Profit You Want

Total dollars from Figure 5.3 (personal budget)   _____

Total dollars from Figure 5.4 (real estate budget)   _____

Dreams/fun   _____

      Total $ needed to cover total expenses   ☐

      Desired profit   _____

      Grand total of dollars you want to earn   ☐

Objectives Don't Stop with Dollars

In my book *How about a Career in Real Estate?* I discussed the expectations of new agents versus the realities. Through surveys with hundreds of new agents, I found that most agents had very high monetary expectations for their first year in the real estate business—expectations that few first-year agents reach. I also discovered that these first-year agents had no idea how to translate the dollars they expected into measurable objectives.

 What do you have to accomplish to get those dollars? To create a plan that you can follow, you must translate the money into *real estate activities.*

Measuring Real Estate Objectives

Until you know how many houses you must sell to earn your desired income, you cannot create a business plan. In real estate, houses sold are called *revenue units. Translating* your dollar income into units allows you to get closer to a plan that guides you in your everyday real estate activities. What is your average commission per unit? Divide that into your monetary goal, and you will know how many houses you need to sell next year. Figure 5.7 takes you through this process. Note that it also asks you to

Figure 5.6

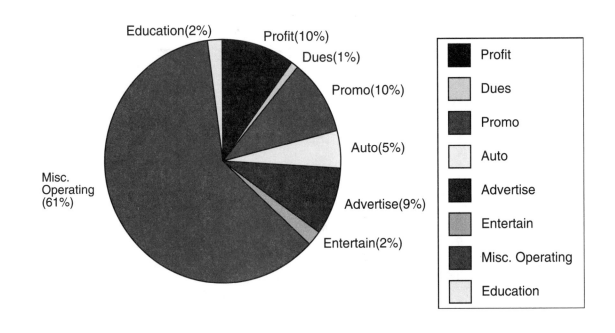

Total Real Estate Operating Budget

Education(2%) Profit(10%)
Dues(1%)
Promo(10%)
Auto(5%)
Advertise(9%)
Entertain(2%)
Misc. Operating (61%)

Legend: Profit, Dues, Promo, Auto, Advertise, Entertain, Misc. Operating, Education

divide your business between listings sold and sales. This important step sets the stage for your marketing plan.

Multiplying Units

All experienced salespeople tell me that more than half their business (some up to 85 percent) come from *referral business*. That is, they do business with people they know. Think of each of those units as a person—a person with a smiling face. Focusing on *happy units* helps you to build a successful career based on high customer service—a key to success in the '90s. To create a powerful business, it is more important to sell homes to a lot of people than to sell two million-dollar homes a year and collect two large commissions. As I did research for the *Career* book, I discovered some figures from NAR that suggested that most agents focus on the wrong objectives. According to NAR's latest survey, agents have increased their median incomes by $5,000 in the last six years (from $17,500 to $22,500). However, their average number of happy customers and clients has shrunk from 16 to less than 14.

Figure 5.7

Objectives: From Dollars to Revenue Units

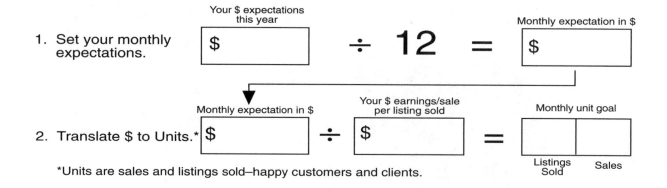

1. Set your monthly expectations.

Your $ expectations this year

$ ÷ 12 =

Monthly expectation in $

$

2. Translate $ to Units.*

Monthly expectation in $

$ ÷

Your $ earnings/sale per listing sold

$ =

Monthly unit goal

Listings Sold | Sales

*Units are sales and listings sold—happy customers and clients.

This means that agents are not creating a solid foundation for referral-return business. Changing the focus from dollars to units results in your creating a powerful, effective long-term business plan.

Refining Your Unit Objectives

Now, let's investigate some principles of setting unit objectives. Figure 5.8 helps you refine your objectives and set specific monthly goals. When creating your unit objectives, remember three important points:

1. *Not every unit sold results in $.* Every sale does not close. When figuring your unit objectives, decide how many units will not close ("sale fails"). Then express your unit and monetary objectives in *total net units and dollars.*

2. *Some listings don't sell.* What was your conversion rate of listings taken to listings sold last year? What are your goals this year? Since only a listing *sold* counts as a revenue unit, be sure to figure your net revenue units on the listing side.

3. *To all sales there is a season.* Figure 5.9 asks you to project your listings, listings sold, sales and referrals out over time. This will help you translate these figures into your daily, weekly and monthly

schedules and, more importantly, plan the intensity of your efforts toward optimum results. Some agents drift most of the year, then get serious about their business in September. However, as Figure 5.10 demonstrates, real estate sales are seasonal. The biggest month for sales is March because people want to buy in time to close and move after school is out. The second busiest month is August since buyers want to finalize their move before school starts. Consciously planning the contour of your business consciously helps you schedule the right daily activities *during the right months.* Figure 5.11 provides some tips on setting objectives.

What's Measured and Why

To expand your business, you need to set objectives in four areas:

1. Listings taken
2. Listings sold
3. Sales
4. Referrals out

By setting objectives, you create measuring sticks of your business. They are also easily quantifiable. In addition, you can create other tracking methods to set *mini-objectives* for the activities you need to complete to reach these objectives (activities such as prospecting, listing presentations, showings—all activities that lead to a sale). Figure 5.12 shows the "business path," the business-producing activities that lead to $$$—the activities you manage and measure to create results.

Who's Your Manager?

Years ago I was a student in a management class of agents who were interested in going into management. I'll never forget Oakley Goodner, one of the all-time great real estate instructors, asking us, "Who's your manager?" Most of us blithely wrote the name of our branch manager. A few smart ones wrote their own names.

One of a manager's functions is to be the agent's business consultant. Another is to provide the agent with the analytical tools needed to *self-manage.* The agent, an independent businessperson, has everything to gain by managing his or her own career. When both agent and manager communicate with these tools, they can work in true partnership to create a dynamic business.

Figure 5.8

Overall Objectives

Name: _____

Office: _____

Date Completed: _____

For Year: _____

Your average commission per sale/listing sold (S/LS) = $ _____

Your past year's ratio of sales written to sales closed _____ %   Your past year's ratio of LT/LS= _____ %

Your next year's desired ratio _____ %   Your next year's ratio of listings sold to sales _____ %

Listings:

Number of listings taken (units) _____

Number of listings sold (units) _____ x average commission _____ = $ _____ − sales fails ($ _____) = $ _____
net income

Sales:

Number of sales (units) _____ x average commission = $ _____ − sales fails ($ _____) = $ _____
net income

Referrals out:

Number of referrals (units) _____ x average commission = $ _____ − sales fails ($ _____) = $ _____
net income

Totals:

Total net revenue units + (LS/S) = [_____]

Total net commissions paid = $ _____ [*]

L = Listing   * paid in that year
LS = Listing Sold   + a revenue unit = a listing sold or a sale
S = Sale

Figure 5.9

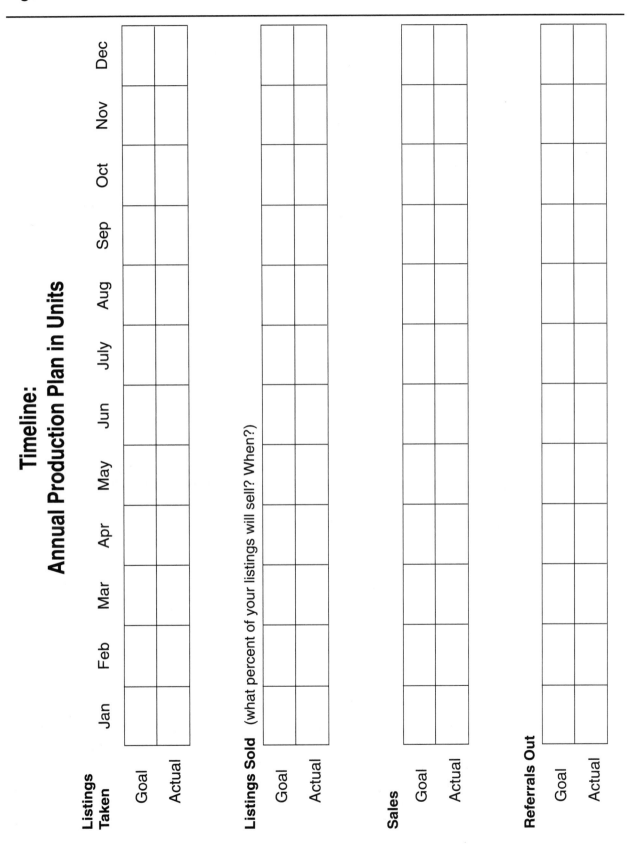

Timeline:
Annual Production Plan in Units

Figure 5.10

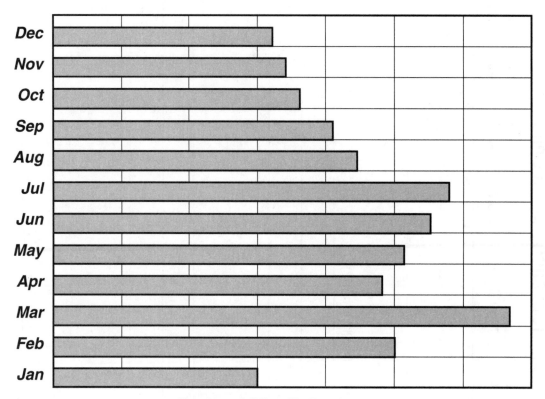

Seasonal Buying Trends

Below are the seasonal trends* to show when buyers purchase homes.
These are *offers to purchase,* not closings. Buyers make buying decisions so they can
close and move in during the months of June and September.

Number of Offers To Purchase

* From a five-year study of purchase and sale agreements by a real estate company

---

How the Numbers Work (Mini-Objectives)

For some of you, this may be a review. But, in my experience, many agents are not familiar with how overall objectives and mini-objectives work or have never looked at them as self-analytical tools.

 The idea is this: The activities you complete each day control your results. Say that you want to make $24,000 this year. What does that mean in units? If your average commission per unit is $2,000, you need to complete 12 net transactions this year. Let's say that you intend for 6 of

Figure 5.11

Tips on Creating Objectives

Objectives must:

- Fit your big-picture goals
- Be attainable
- Be expressed as revenue units
- Be planned over time
- Be related to mini-objectives
- Be monitored and measured

those to be listings sold and 6 to be sales. Now, what does that have to do with your daily activities? First, you need to understand *mini-objectives*. Let's work backwards from sales to daily activities. Let's say you want to sell one home per month. According to national statistics, you will need to put people in your car eight times. That doesn't mean that you put one group of people in your car eight times, but that you show homes eight times in one month. It's simply the law of averages. Now where do you find enough qualified people to put in your car eight times in one month? You prospect—a good number to call on monthly is 400 to start. From plenty of good potential prospects, you can put the *best* prospects in your car—the ones who'll buy from you now. To accomplish this, schedule 100 sales calls per week, and attempt to get from your prospecting three qualifying appointments and two showing appointments. A caveat: You must work the numbers long enough to take advantage of the law of averages. Our son Chris is a fine basketball player. He has a 58 percent three-point shooting average. But he had a dry spell, where he went 0 for 17. He didn't quit shooting. Now he's back on track. You should never quit prospecting, qualifying or showing!

On the listing side: Let's say you want to list one home per month to sell in normal market time. How many *prospects* will you need to talk to in order to find enough *qualified prospects* to ensure one *qualified listing* that will sell in normal market time? Here are probabilities. You need to talk to 100 prospects a week to secure three listing appointments to list one

Figure 5.12

The Business Path

Below is the business path—the path that agents follow to create sales. It starts with prospecting and ends with the close. The more times agents complete these activities, the more money they make.

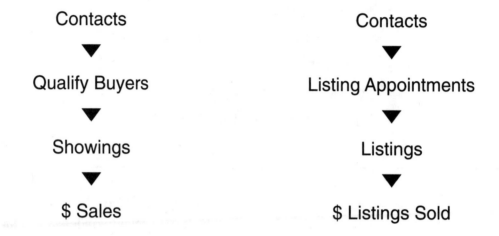

Contacts	Contacts
▼	▼
Qualify Buyers	Listing Appointments
▼	▼
Showings	Listings
▼	▼
$ Sales	$ Listings Sold

marketable property. These ratios could vary in your market area. Ask top agents in your office about their prospecting, qualifying and listing ratios. Then set your *mini-objectives,* and log them into your daily calendar.

Measuring Your Results for Self-Management

As you set your goals and complete your activities, you will discover two things:

1. You will develop your own ratios of success—and can set some new standards to beat yourself. This is a great time-management tool.

2. You will create the analytical tools to get on track and stay on track. If you get off track again, you will immediately be able to see where,

when and how you created poorer results than you expected. With that information, you can consult with your manager for a change in your plan. Dan was an experienced agent, but he was in a slump. He went to his manager for guidance. Because the manager knew sales ratios, he asked Dan how many groups of people Dan had shown homes to in the past three months. Dan told his manager that he had been very busy, that he had shown homes to groups of people 25 times in the past three months but had not made a sale. If you were Dan's manager, what would you guess is wrong? It could be that Dan was not qualifying buyers or that he was not asking for the order (closing buyers). Because Dan's manager analyzed the numbers Dan provided, he and Dan discovered the root of the problem and created a plan to increase Dan's ability to qualify buyers. Dan pulled out of the slump and set mini-objectives, measured results and made adjustments in his business plan. Now he self-manages his activities.

My program *Up and Running in 30 Days* provides a model plan for the new agent, prioritizes activities and teaches how to monitor a start-up plan. In addition, there are step-by-step weekly plans—all prioritized—and an "accomplishments" summary. To help new agents learn *how* to work their plans, I provide six audiotapes with business planning guidelines and actual role-plays of sales calls and sales skills. If you want more in-depth information on self-managing by the numbers, it's in this program. (See the Reference section for more information on this program.) In Chapter 7, you will find a form for setting goals and keeping track of actual sales calls in specific target markets (prospecting).

Putting It All Together

Figure 5.13 is a timeline—a way for you to see how your activities ensure your results. You can see the variable that most agents miss—*time*. As you plot your activities to results, be realistic about how long it will take to find, work with and close buyers. How long will it take to find, list and sell your listings? How long will it take from the time you sell a home to the time it closes and you get a check? On the expense side: Log in your total business expenses (operating and marketing). Put down your earned income (when you make a sale or your listing sells) and paid income (when you get a check), in the months you think it will occur. Figure your profit per month and your profit to date.

Now you have a complete picture of how your activities, income and expenses create your break-even point (the point at which your expenses equal your income) and your profit per month and year to date.

Figure 5.13

Timeline: Activities, Results, Expenses, Income Break-Even, Profit

1. Estimate your activities and when they will create income.

Activity/Income: Month	Jan	Feb	Mar	Apr	May	June	July	Aug	Sep	Oct	Nov	Dec	Total
Closings													
Sales													
Listings sold													
Listings secured													
Showings													
Listing presentations													
Face-to-face contacts													

2. Tally your expenses per month. Log in your projected earnings and "paids" (closings).

	Jan	Feb	Mar	Apr	May	June	July	Aug	Sep	Oct	Nov	Dec	Total
Business expenses													
Earned income (written)													
Paid income (closed)													
Profit per month													
Profit (year-to-date)													

Reprinted with permission: *Up and Running in 30 Days*, ©1993 by Carla Cross Seminars. Published by Carla Cross Seminars, Issaquah, WA. All rights reserved.

Figure 5.14

Activities, Expenses, Results, Profits

1. Estimate your activities and when they will create income. Start with face-to-face contacts.

Activity/Income: Month	Jan	Feb	Mar	Apr	May	June	July	Aug	Sep	Oct	Nov	Dec	Total
Closings				▲1	▲1	▲1							
Sales		1	1	1	▲1	▲1							
Listings sold					1	1							
Listings secured	1		1		1								
Showings	3	3	8	8	8	8							
Listing presentations	2	2	2	2	2	2							
Face-to-face contacts	400	300	300	100	100	100							

2. Tally your expenses per month. Log in your projected earnings and "paids" (closings).

Business expenses	1,149	748	818	748	888	818							
Earned income (written)	0	1,500	1,500	0	3,000	3,000							
Paid income (closed)	0	0	0	1,500	1,500	1,500							

Profit per month	($1,149)	($748)	($818)	$752	$612	$682

At the end of six months, this new agent is almost at break-even.

Figure 5.14 shows how a new agent plotted her activities, results, expenses and income through time to find out her break-even and profit picture. In Chapter 11, *goal* and *actual* are added to the grid, so you can use this grid to set goals and keep track of your successes.

Becoming More Effective

Besides doing lots of business activities, you can increase your bottom line by *becoming more effective* at these activities.

In your situation analysis, you discovered your rates of effectiveness in several areas. For example, you found out what percent of your listings taken actually sell. Figure 5.15 sets objectives for increasing the effectiveness of your business. As you decide on these numbers, think about how you will change your business practices. Many activities will be outlined in the professional development section of your plan. For example, let's say you want to change your ratio of listings taken to listings sold from 50 percent to 80 percent. You may decide to take a listing course, buy a book or tape, interview successful agents, etc. Increasing your skill helps you to increase your business effectiveness, which directly impacts your productivity and profitability.

Overall Plan Summary

Now that you have considered the "big picture" part of your plan, it's helpful to summarize the main intent of your plan. You may want to do this in terms of this year's plan or in terms of an even bigger picture—two to three years. If you are in your first year of business, summarize by saying you intend to "create the foundation for a high-producing career while making a minimum of $24,000 this first year." In Appendix A there are two sample plans with plan summaries. Use the worksheet in Figure 5.16 to summarize your plan.

Summary

You have completed the journey through objectives. First, you grasped the big picture of your life objectives. You put your real estate objectives into that picture. Then you computed your expenses and added the amount you wanted to profit. This completed your monetary goals—laying the groundwork to meaningful real estate goals. As you translated your monetary goals into units, you created measurable objectives that guide

Figure 5.15

Setting Objectives for Sales Effectiveness

Of all the areas that you analyzed and want to change and/or improve, which are the most important to you to increase your business effectiveness?

☐ Change ratio of listings taken to listings sold from_____ % to _____ %.

☐ Change ratio of listings sold to sales from _____ % to _____ %.

☐ Change listing time on market from _____ average days to _____ average days.

☐ Increase average commission by changing price range for listings from $ _____ to $ _____ .

☐ Change price range for sales to increase average commission from $ _____ to $ _____ .

☐ Reduce number of showings per sale to _____ .

☐ Change ratio of listing presentations to listings that sell from _____ % to _____ %.

☐ Switch from _____ % proactive methods to find buyers/sellers to _____ %.

These priorities for your overall sales strategy will provide the basis for your marketing and professional development plans.

---

you as you implement your business plan. To get closer to *self-management*, you broke down your unit goals into *mini-objectives*. You created goals for increased business effectiveness. With those objectives, you put the whole picture back together, with the break-even flowchart and your plan summary. Now, you're ready to create dynamic action plans to reach your goals.

Figure 5.16

Plan Summary

My main concern at this point in my career is to: _____

_____

_____

_____

_____

_____

_____

My plan will assure I accomplish this because: _____

_____

_____

_____

_____

_____

_____

My overall interest this year is to: _____

_____

_____

_____

_____

_____

_____

CHAPTER

6

Marketing: The Action Plan To Grow Your Business

"The way this system pictorially shows how to spend my marketing time and dollars has really benefited me in organizing my business."

—Lorna Willard

In This Chapter ·

Segmenting your market

Determining your best target markets

Evaluating market potential

From Thoughts to Actions

You have explored the state of your market and your vision for your business, and you have decided on your desired end results. Now you are ready to hone in on action plans to reach your objectives—your way. To clarify and relate activities to the big picture, let's divide these action plans into two sections:

1. Marketing (includes personal marketing)
2. Personal Development (reaching business objectives through training, hiring assistants, support services, etc.)

In the marketing part of the action plan, you will create an overall marketing strategy, identify where you will go to get your business and create the tactical moves (everyday activities) that will help you to get

Figure 6.1

Your Marketing Plan: Targets and Tactics

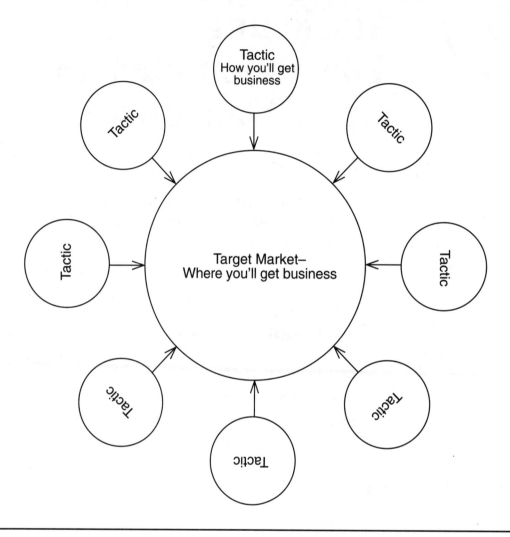

business from your best sources. This is, by the way, where personal marketing fits into your business planning scheme. Figure 6.1 illustrates the relationships between target and tactics. The center circle represents *where* you will get your business. The outer circles represent *how* you will communicate with these potential sources of business.

Segmenting Your Market

☞   Generally, agents make one important mistake when they create their marketing plans: Agents think they should try to communicate with *everyone* in their market areas. However, as we discussed previously, trying to communicate with everyone effectively communicates with *no one* in today's marketing world. You can narrow your scope by *segmenting* your market into groupings with common characteristics. Then you can communicate with each group according to what is important to that particular group. In the marketing world, general groups (people or places) are segmented by clustering them according to their:

- common *demographics*—age, family members, income, etc.
- common *psychographics*—life habits (religion, beliefs, habits)

In real estate, sources of business that have common segments are:

- past customers/clients
- geographical area
- for-sale-by-owners
- expired listings
- first-time buyers
- move-up buyers
- builders
- transferees
- specific professions (e.g., attorneys)
- retirees

 Because these sources can be pinpointed and targeted for specific marketing tactics, these sources are termed *target markets*. (Note: They are always geographical areas or people—never activities. Keep this in mind as we further develop the idea of target market and tactics.)

Determining Your Best Target Markets for Increased Business

To expand your business with the least effort, pick the best potential markets. But what determines *best*? Following are four criteria for determining the best markets:

1. Markets that cost you the least amount of money for the greatest return on your investment.
2. Markets that cost you the least in terms of *personal price*. That is, the markets that yield a high response to your sales calls, the markets where people trust you easily, the markets where people follow your real estate advice for their best interests.
3. Markets where you can compete with other agents—and win with reasonable financial and personal cost.

4. Markets that have been the best sources of sales and listings sold for you in the past.

Using these criteria, go back to your earlier business analysis of the past year. What was your best market for sales and listings leads? Put these sources inside the circles on Figure 6.2. If you are an experienced agent, you probably found that your best source of sales and listings sold was *personal referrals*. If not, your goal is to create a business where these people are your best source of leads. You should make personal referrals your best source for three important reasons:

1. It's a less expensive way to get leads. According to marketing surveys, *it costs six times as much to get a new customer than to get a previous one.*
2. It's easier. Past customers and clients are more pleasant to deal with—you know them, and they know you. By working with them, you retain a high sense of self-esteem—a necessary quality for success.
3. Past customers and clients are loyal. You do not have to work as hard to retain your investment in them.

According to a NAR survey (see Figure 6.3), referrals to agents account for 41.8 percent of their sales. In talking to experienced agents, they actually set goals for 75 to 90 percent of their business to come from previous customers and clients—or people they already know. I don't mean to suggest that your past customers and clients will automatically return five to ten years later. Nor do I suggest that they will, on their own, refer large numbers of clients to you. To get value from your circle of influence and previous clients, you must work them just like any other target market by frequently and consistently communicating with them.

Agents Miss This Target's Value

When I created and conducted educational programs for a large independent real estate company, I frequently was asked to help agents create *personal marketing programs*. I found that many agents took the wrong initial approach to expanding their businesses. They thought that they should create programs to communicate with *strangers* and ignored their best sources for business—previous customers or clients.

Betty's thought process illustrates the point. Betty wanted help in creating a marketing program to increase her business. She had been an agent in the area for over ten years. Her productivity was always $4 million or more in sales volume. Although she steadily maintained her business, she wanted to step up to the next level of productivity. To do this, Betty

Figure 6.2

Choose Your Target Markets

1. Fill in the top portion of each circle with a name of a potential target (past customers and clients, geographical farm, FSBO, expired listings, certain professions, etc.).

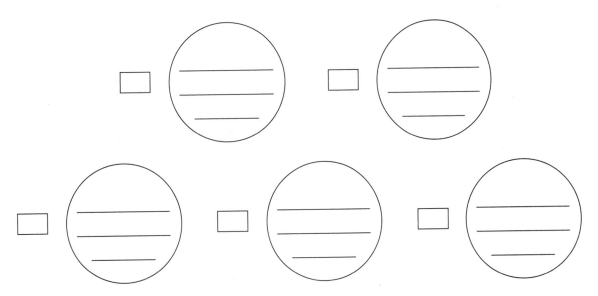

2. Estimate the number of potential contacts in each market by filling the middle blank in each circle (prospecting).

3. Estimate the number of listings sold and sales derived from this market by filling in the bottom portion of the circle.

4. Prioritize the importance of these markets to you by numbering the market in the box (#1 is your best market).

Example:

Figure 6.3

Where Buyers Come From*

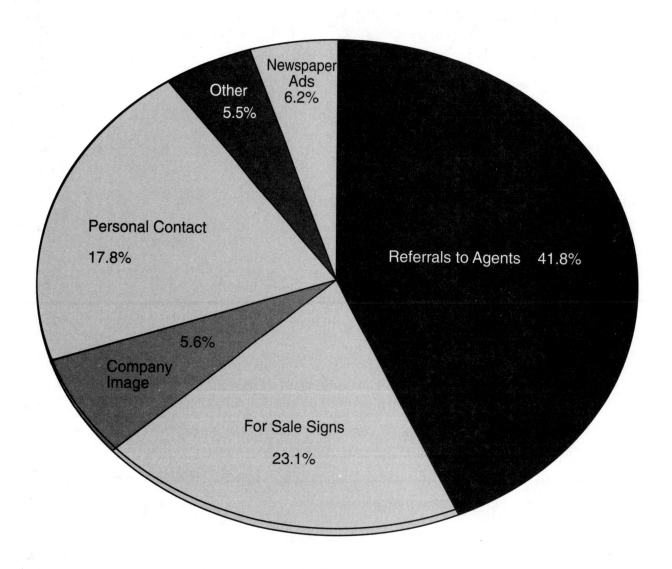

*From a survey completed by the National Association of REALTORS®

realized she needed some marketing programs. She had a great idea that would *only* cost her $10,000 that next year. She would advertise in a homes-for-sale magazine, using her newly created slogan, "When you're ready, call Betty." When I asked her why she had chosen this vehicle, she said that it seemed to provide the best way to "get her name out." Realizing that $10,000 was a lot of money to spend on communicating with "generic strangers," I asked her to describe her total marketing plan, starting with her best source of customers—her past clients. She told me that she was doing a great job with them—she communicated twice a year! What a pity. Betty had literally hundreds of satisfied customers who would *love* to give her referrals—if only they knew she wanted them. Betty had missed her best source of business because she did not understand the two most important marketing principles in marketing/business planning:

1. Narrow your field to communicate meaningfully with people—the target market approach.

2. Build a strong distribution plan to communicate with your *best market*—people who already know and care about you—people who already have a good image of you as a real estate professional.

Think of Previous Clients as a "Farm"

You wouldn't think of calling on homeowners in an area only once a year—not if you expected to get some business from them. Yet it is amazing how little time and effort agents expend on their best source of business—previous clients. Treating this source of business as a viable target market has proven rewards. A study by the Personal Marketing Company of Houston showed that, if agents simply *mailed* a newsletter to previous customers *twice a year*, they would increase their chances of a relist by 45 percent! In addition to direct relists and repurchases from this market, you have many opportunities of referrals from these satisfied customers and clients.

Figure 6.4 demonstrates the power of multiplying your referrals from this best source. I discovered this firsthand—by counting the buyers and sellers generated from one seller. To my awe, the number totaled seven! And I had not worked this source nearly as well as I could have. In Chapter 7, we will discuss specific tactics that you can use to communicate with your best target market to get relists, repurchases and powerful referrals. If you understand the two marketing principles discussed above, the tactical choices become easy. When you know *what* market to impact first and the *results* you want from that market, you can decide on the specific messages you want to communicate to that market.

Figure 6.4

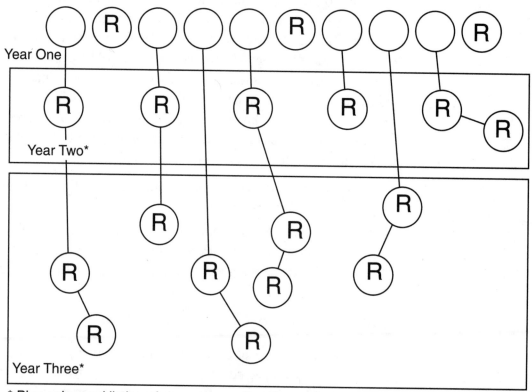

How Referrals Multiply Your Business

Year One

Year Two*

Year Three*

* Plus sales and listings from sources other than referrals

R = Referral
Open Circles = Other Business

Evaluating Market Potential

We have discussed the potential of your best target market—previous customers and clients—and some criteria for choosing target markets. Market potential can also be evaluated through *market research.* You can estimate the value of listings and sales to determine that the financial and human resources that you commit to each market are good investments. Without this research, you could make poor marketing decisions. One day I was talking to an agent who had been in the business for two years. He wanted to "farm" a geographical area called Somerset. Since he had not done any market research, he had no idea of the potential business—or of the competition. However, I knew that a husband-wife team had expended tens of thousands of dollars and three years to capture a dominant market share in Somerset. The team would be difficult and costly to battle for market position. I suggested that the agent do market research to determine potential and competition. He returned with a decision to invest in a "farm" that was "unowned."

To research the value of a geographical farm, there are three steps:

1. *Determine your market potential.*
   - Find out the number of listings now in your defined area.
   - Determine the percent of those listings that have sold in the last 12 months.
   - Determine normal market time.
   - Tally the companies, offices and agents who control the market in the area.
   - Decide who is your competition and their relative strength.

2. *Determine your potential income.*
   - Figure out the number of listings that you can control.
   - Compute the percent of the listings that will sell.
   - Decide on the commission dollars per sale, and multiply that by the number of listings you will sell and sales that result from farming the area.

3. *Figure your net dollars from your investment.*
   - Estimate the amount of money you will spend that year on your farming efforts.
   - Subtract that amount from your estimated gross income to get the net dollars on your investment.

Ask yourself: Is my investment in this area worth it for my gross and net income? Figure 6.5 shows an example of a farm projection and evaluation. In addition, there are worksheets in the Chapter 7 that will help you project and measure investment potential.

Comparing Income Potential of Various Target Markets

Using Figure 6.2, estimate the number of potential contacts you have in each target market (use the middle blank in each circle). Next, estimate the number of listings sold and sales derived from this market by filling in the bottom portion of the circle. Last, prioritize the importance of these

Figure 6.5

Example:
Potential Profit from a Farm

Number of homes: 300
Listings past year: 30
Listings sold: 15

I can list: 4 the first year of working this market.
               3 will sell and close.

3 x $3,000 (my average commission) = $9,000 total commissions

Budget: $1,000

Evaluation: Good expenditure for return, especially to
               establish my dominance in this area

markets to you by numbering each market in the box. The total number of listings and sales should be the total number of listings sold and sales you expect from your *proactive* marketing efforts.

These results, along with any listings sold and sales from open houses or floor time, should equal the total number of listings sold and sales you expect to attain next year (the number that you totaled in the section on overall objectives). For example, let's say you want 12 of your listings sold next year, and you expect 12 sales. Breaking that down further, you expect 6 of those sales and 6 of those listings sold to come from past customers and clients, 3 of those listings sold and 3 sales from your geographical farm, and 3 of those listings sold and 3 sales to come from floor time and open house. You have now pinpointed the origination of your results. With that breakdown, you have an excellent start to build action plans around your best target markets. You know the potential of each market, and you have prioritized the importance of each of your markets.

Using Your Business Research as a Power Tool

Since you are now an accomplished market researcher, let me show you another way to use the information. It has been my experience that sellers expect advertising and open houses because they think these marketing tactics sell homes—in particular, their home, although this has not proved to be the case. It is true that advertising and open houses generate leads, but these people must be qualified and shown the right homes. The home advertised is rarely the home that particular caller purchases. To get this point across, use the worksheet in Figure 6.6. First, tally all your buyers and trace back to where you first met them. (If you don't have enough buyers, ask others in your office to participate.) Then review how the buyers found their homes. A few years ago, a large real estate company researched 100 out-of-town, transferred buyers and found that more than 90 percent of the buyers had been referred to the agent with whom they later purchased their homes. And in more than 95 percent of the purchases, the *agent found the home and showed it to the purchasers—through the multiple listing service.* Not one purchaser found the home through an open house or advertising. Your research will likely show similar results. Armed with that information, you can design an effective marketing plan for the seller and show him or her why you are marketing first to *agents,* not to the *public.*

Summary

You used market research to find out your best target markets. You gathered information to assess the potential of new target markets and to calculate the return on your investment. You divided your sales objectives amongst your target markets to determine your desired results from each market. Now you are ready to design marketing tactics (promotions) to communicate with and get sales results from each market.

Figure 6.6

Your Best Source of Business and How Customers Found the Home They Bought

Name_____ Office_____ Date_____

Customer Name _____

Address _____

Price of Home Purchased _____ Area _____

First Met: (Circle multiple selections)

☐ Newspaper Ad Call
Block*   Scatter*

☐ Sign Call

☐ Magazine
"Homes" Magazine
Your Local Magazine

☐ Referral
Called me   I called customers

☐ Open House
Ad   Sign

☐ Marketing To Target
Newsletter   Direct mail
Brochure   Specialty
Personal call

☐ Relocation

☐ Other (Explain)
_____
_____

Found the home they bought by:

_____
_____
_____
_____
_____
_____
_____

Comments:

_____
_____
_____
_____

Ad Calls:
* Block is large ad
* 'Scatter' or Spot ad is individual ad

Note: Use your individual newspaper names to clarify ad calls as precisely as possible. On personal marketing, you may add further categories.

Promotional Idea: Use this market research to show sellers the best targets for their homes—and how buyers find the home they purchase.

CHAPTER

7

Tactics:
How To Make
Your Move

"Thinking in terms of 'circle planning' around a target market, planning tactics and creating a budget makes your business more efficient and effective."

—Duncan Clark

In This Chapter •

Tactical moves: Your choices

Developing your tactics

Measuring and evaluating your tactics

Two kinds of advertising—and when to use each

You have patiently worked through the *thought* part of the planning process. You have your vision of success, and you have developed some overall objectives. In addition, you have selected the best markets to expand your business. Is this process different than you imagined? Many real estate agents think of the planning process as two steps:

1. Naming their monetary goals

2. Deciding on the actions to get to their goals

The problem with this approach is that it leaves *you* out. Making decisions about what actions to take without considering the state of *your* market, *your* business and *your* talents is difficult. That is why you analyzed, researched and evaluated potential business decisions. With all that information and with *great confidence*, you can choose the actions that will help you reach your marketing objectives.

Business planners and marketers call the everyday, specific activities that impact our target market *tactics.* Following are examples of tactics:

- For a geographical farm: *Agent knocks on doors six times a year—no cost.*

- For previous customers and clients: *Agent sends a postcard (written by agent and prepared by assistant) three times a year—cost approximately $500 for mailing list of 1,000.*

To work in *your* marketing plan, tactics need to:

- relate to your overall business strategy (more on that in Chapter 8);
- relate to your market conditions;
- connect with each target market;
- relate to each other over time;
- have time frames assigned (to go into your daily planner); and
- have a person assigned to complete each task.

A Secret to Creating Tactics: Creativity before Criticism

One of an agent's favorite replies to suggestions about tactics is: *It won't work for me in my market.* Of course, no action works exactly the same way for each agent in each market. But an agent's job is to look at the *possibilities* that tactical ideas represent. Thinking through the prior part of the planning process provides perspective to *make actions work for each of us in each of our markets.* What I am suggesting is that you apply the same creative process to your business plan that a musician or artist applies to creating a work of art. After all, when you get done with your plan, it should represent the essence of *you.* Artists understand the years of evolving creativity that go into a unique expression of a painting or a piece of music. My background in music gave me an opportunity to view the creative process. I studied working manuscripts of great composers, such as Beethoven, that demonstrated how great minds work to consider, experiment, evolve and re-create. To compose a sonata, Beethoven wrote and scribbled, corrected and rewrote, wrote and scribbled again. His works evolved over a period of time, becoming more complex and "dark" as he grew older.

Think of your business plan in the same way. You must write and scribble, try ideas, improvise, evolve—create and re-create. As Beethoven began his career, no one could have told him how his music would sound after 15 years of composing and evolving. In fact, it wouldn't have been any fun for Beethoven to have known! What spurred Beethoven to compose and evolve his compositions was his belief in himself to be able to compose music. He didn't scribble a few notes and give up. He recognized his musical talent, fueled his desire to create and *kept at it.*

Take a lesson from Beethoven: *Keep creativity away from judgment* as you consider the actions you will take to make your plan live through your daily activities. To get that sense of confidence in your abilities that Beethoven had, use the business planning process in this book, which will increase your *intuitive sense* about your talents, strengths and abilities. Then, as you choose your tactics, you will be amazed at how certain tactics reach out and seem to choose you! Just as Beethoven heard melodies in his head before he saw them on paper, you will think through tactical possibilities and create cohesive plans faster and faster as you repeat the creative planning process over a period of years.

Tactical Moves: Your Choices

Just as Beethoven had all 88 keys and thousands of combinations of those keys to draw from for his compositions, you have literally thousands of choices as you decide on your tactical moves. In this chapter, I will provide some guidelines to help you make your choices. First, let's simply look at how marketers divide our choices.

In the marketing world, tactical choices are called *promotions.* Within that category are four subcategories:

1. Personal selling
2. Public relations
3. Advertising
4. Sales promotion

Personal selling is getting in front of people. Honing your sales skills increases your chances of personal selling success, as does creating complimentary sales materials, such as listing books and professional portfolios. Public relations consists of promotional moves like press releases, news articles and interviews. Advertising is best-known, and the largest percent of a real estate company's promotional dollars is spent here. This includes newspaper, radio and television advertising to promote products, services or the image of the advertiser. Finally, sales promotion includes all the newsletters, flyers, brochures and what real estate market-ers call "trinkets and trash"—key chains, cups, pens, etc.

Figure 7.1

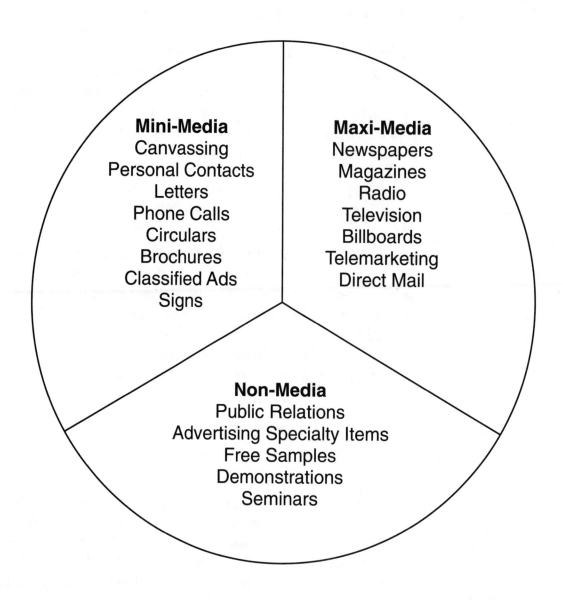

Your Promotional Choices

Tactics Categorized by Cost

Rather than stick with the academic view of promotional choices, let's look at those choices differently. Agents have limited budgets; they need to get the "biggest bang for their buck." So, let's group all the promotional choices into three categories—loosely by promotional cost:

1. Mini-media
2. Maxi-media
3. Non-media

Figure 7.1 shows the possibilities in each category. Which category is the least expensive? Which category is the most expensive? Which category is the most labor-intensive? Which category rates the highest in believability from your consumers? In this chapter and in Chapter 8, you will investigate the choices in each category in relation to your career development, your marketing dollars and your overall marketing strategy.

Tactics in Relation to Your Career Development

Recently, I was listening to an audiotape of top producers as they explained their promotional tactics. These agents complete an average of 150 transactions per year. As you can imagine, their promotional choices were much different from those choices of a first-year agent or a mid-career agent.

Yet, *their first choice of target market was the same.* The major recurrent theme was: *Remind past customers and clients or people you know that you're in the real estate business.* Your first decision regarding your tactics is to choose the methods that communicate best with your best target market—your previous customers and clients. And, if you're too new to have many past clients, start with people you already know. A promotional tactic by a superstar might be a full-page newspaper ad thanking his or her customers and clients for a great year (at a cost of several thousand dollars). If you're a relatively new agent, you might translate this "thank you" tactic into sending a postcard to all the people you know, thanking them for their support that year (at a cost of only a few hundred dollars).

In translating the idea of a tactic from superstar to you (and your budget), the important point is to figure out what that tactic will accomplish. Then create a tactic within your budget and experience level to get the same result that the superstar's tactic accomplished.

Promotional Tactics To Spread the News

☞   The second recurrent theme of the superstars was: *Promote yourself based on your successes.* For example, multimillion dollar agent Nada Sundermeyer promotes her success record as a listing agent to sellers whose listings have expired. On the expiration date, Nada sends a letter to the seller, relating her phenomenal sales record with expired listings. She asks the seller what kind of representation the seller wants. Of course, the seller wants a listing agent who gets results. Nada has the desired record, as she reminds the seller. This letter is so strong that sellers actually call Nada—but only if they're serious about selling their homes. How does Nada get them to call? She relies on her sales record of success. It's the most powerful tool she—or any agent—has. Again and again on the audiotape, superstars stated that they made every business decision based on whether it added or detracted from their success record. They realized that they could not promote themselves based on their failures!

But how often do agents take an over-priced listing that results in low levels of customer satisfaction and wasted promotional dollars—and actually *decreases* their images as successful agents? How often do agents fail to qualify buyers, so that they can't sell them the homes—disappointing them and decreasing their images as a successful real estate agents? Your first step in creating promotional tactics that work is to create job *habits* that ensure your success record. In Chapter 9, you will work at setting performance objectives to guarantee top sales records—so that you will have something meaningful to promote.

Create Relationships within Your Desired Market

☞   Creating effective tactics is simple if you create tactics market by market. Then keep all the marketing relationships in perspective. I am referring to relationships of:

- target market to tactic (be sure the tactic is appropriate for the market);
- tactic to tactic (be sure the tactics relate one to another); and
- you to the target market and tactics (it's like you to communicate this way).

Figure 7.2 shows the thought process needed to ensure that you consider all these relationships as you create your tactics. If you fail to keep these relationships in mind, you can waste valuable monetary and personal resources.

Figure 7.2

Targets and Tactics: Relationships

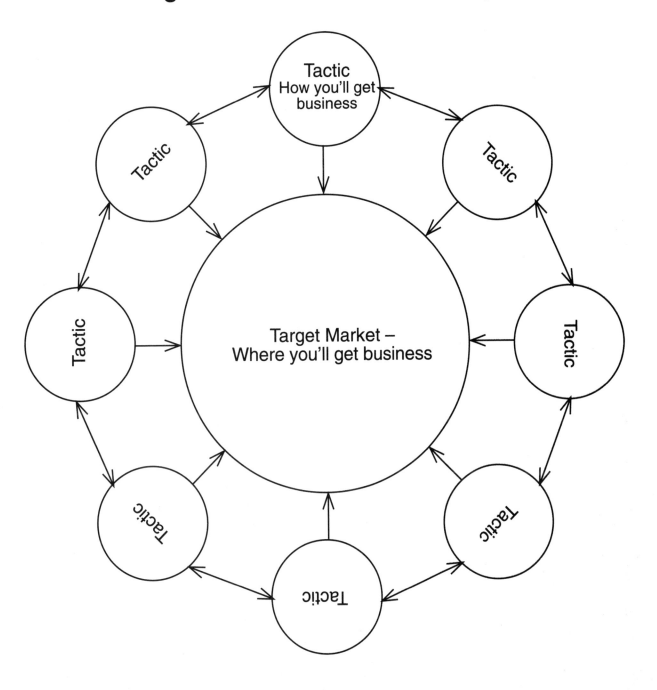

When a Tactic Doesn't Relate to a Specific Market

Sally created a personal brochure. But after she had thousands printed, she did not know who to give or send it to. Because she had no target market in mind when she created the brochure, her message was very generic. Sally had created a print piece with no *action* for it. The brochures ended up under her desk and in her car trunk. If Sally had started with a particular target market and *then* decided on how to communicate with it, she could have concluded that a brochure could communicate with several of her markets. Then she could have designed a meaningful message, enhanced her image in her particular markets and effectively used her monetary and personal resources.

When Tactics Aren't Related

George decided to create a geographical target—a farm. He did the research and thought that First Meadows would be a good farm area for him. He had heard agents say that you should knock on doors and send information to the farm. So he started knocking on doors and sending information. However, he didn't take the planning time to think through his actions before he started. His actions, therefore, were sporadic and unrelated. Soon he lost interest in his farm because he "got busy." In contrast, at the same time that George established a farm, Rick decided to farm High Meadows, the development right next to First Meadows. Rick planned an overall marketing strategy for his farm, using his assessment of strengths and weaknesses of his competition. He thought through his farm program, deciding on when to call in person, when to mail pieces and when to follow up by phone. His marketing words and written messages related to each other, building on the same theme. At the end of one year, Rick dominated High Meadows. The difference was that Rick put two marketing principles to work that have the most impact on the success of any marketing campaign: *frequency and consistency*. That frequency and consistency is easy to attain if you follow the three rules of relationships:

1. Start with your target market, and create tactics meaningful to that market.

2. Relate tactics to tactics within that market.

3. Relate the tactics to *you*.

This last relationship is so important that we will devote an entire chapter (see Chapter 8) to discussing personalized tactical moves (agents term these *personal marketing*).

Figure 7.3

50 Creative Promotional Tactics
From Successful Agents across the Nation

1. Put a brochure in every envelope you send. Use sections of the brochure for other uses—ads, press releases, etc.

2. Have your manager write a letter of reference. Use in brochure and/or portfolio.

3. Have a famous acquaintance write a letter of reference. Use in brochure and/or portfolio.

4. Become renowned for something by the REALTOR® community. Use in print promotions.

5. Tie in your newsletters with another professional (like a dentist).

6. Develop the team concept and promote it (title, mortgage company, escrow company, etc.).

7. Form a professional lead-exchange group. Meet monthly. Use in your promotions.

8. Put a personalized marketing message at the bottom of every flyer. Distribute to target markets. State your specific, personalized service.

9. Before finishing a brochure, take it to your valued customers/clients for review. Send them a finished copy with a note thanking them and asking them to distribute the brochure to others.

10. Send a change-of-address notice on your personalized stationery to all friends of your sellers (get list from sellers).

11. Use a "media alert" format to get an interview. Work with your marketing director for best results.

12. Volunteer yourself to your manager/owner as a media contact.

13. Put the media on your distribution calendar for all your personalized marketing.

14. As a "thank you" for referrals to you, send flowers to the office of the referral source.

15. Send a letter with your brochure to expired listings—to FSBOs.

16. Make "teaser campaign cards" with little wording to get attention of your target market. Use spaced repetition to distribute.

17. Use press releases at every opportunity—courses taken, conventions attended, new marketing strategies.

18. Survey a target market. Call newspaper for interview on the results.

19. Be an expert on a panel. Write a press release.

20. Multiply yourself. Exchange a difficult customer/client with another agent.

21. Send copies of your press releases to past customers/clients with notes telling them what you're accomplishing.

22. Write an article. Send reprints to all your contacts.

23. Make an audio tape for FSBOs or expireds as part of your personalized marketing program.

24. Bring your brochures to seminars and distribute them. Ask for referrals.

25. Decide on a competitive strategy and "live it" in all your promotions. Example: A fine pianist recorded Christmas music and gave it to all his past customers and clients.

Figure 7.3   Continued

26. Think of previous customers as links to new business. Who do they know that could buy? Example: A farm of 50-year-old to 60-year-old residents have children who could buy. Promote to that need. Create demand!

27. Promote a new service that you created as a result of client demand. Example: Call after every showing to give feedback.

28. Write a column in your local newspaper. Use reprints of your column in your promotions.

29. In your geographical farm: Do historical research and publish a book about the area. Promote these efforts in the press.

30. Use your company-sponsored community service to promote yourself. Have your picture taken at the event. Send with a caption to your target markets.

31. Give magnets with utilities, government phone numbers. Circle prospect with them after a listing presentation.

32. Give pocket calendars, jar openers or a snack clip. These are gifts of value and have a shelf life of five to ten years.

33. Match the gift to the market (first-time homebuyers–something practical).

34. Give a map of the area to new transferees.

35. Give a Christmas tape (perhaps the high school choir) to valued clients/customers.

36. Give the National Association of REALTORS® Home Guide to specific target markets. Suggestion: Put it in hotels.

37. Give kids frisbees.

38. Have custom balloons made with your name. Use at open houses. Give to kids.

39. Offer a seller's kit to FSBOs. Get buyer referrals from FSBOs–even if you don't list the home.

40. Give a homebuyer's kit after your qualifying session with a prospective buyer.

41. Gifts after closing: Give a cookbook of regional dishes.

42. Buyers' or sellers' gifts at closing: Give an artist's rendering of their home. Make notecards that say "compliments of [your name]."

43. Put together a book about buyers' new neighbors. Get information from 20 neighbors. Distribute to 100 people in the area. Ask for referrals.

44. Give a homebuyer's tax kit.

45. Prepare a videotape of the new house for the relocating buyers.

46. Give a binder/large calculator at closing to sellers. Include your business card.

47. Make each gift a part of the whole follow-through program. Deliver it yourself.

48. Give the buyers/sellers keys to their new house on your personalized key ring.

49. Deliver a present personally to your referral source at his/her office. Chat with others there. Give them mementos.

50. Survey past customers for new services. Tell them, then, the new services you're providing. Ask for leads.

Creative Tactical Choices

As I travel around the country as a speaker, I hear many agents' tactical choices. Figure 7.3 provides a list of 50 creative tactical choices successful agents have used to impact their target markets. With the information provided in this chapter, you can start creating *your* tactical moves.

Using the Tactical Planning Sheets

Figure 7.4 is the process I have used with scores of agents to help them choose effective tactics for their particular target markets. It's simple, it follows the guidelines of great marketers, and it keeps all the marketing relationships in perspective. Here are the steps to complete the worksheet:

- Fill in the middle circle.
- Fill in the smaller circles. To effectively impact a market, you need at least six communications per year—balancing in-person, telephone and mail.
- Using the small squares with #, prioritize your tactics. Choose the ones you intend to do. Cross out the rest.
- Add a budget for each tactic.
- Add a date for the tactic to be accomplished, where it says "date." Put this date in your daily schedule.

Now you have created many of your "job activities"—you know what to do each day to create business.

Itemizing Your Tactics for Time Management

In addition to using the "circular" worksheets, some planners like to itemize their tactics in each target market. If you want to see all the tactics and dates for completion on one sheet, use Figure 7.5. Then transfer these tactics to your monthly planning calendar.

Setting Goals and Keeping Track of Sales Calls

One of my favorite truisms is: *The business starts when the salesperson makes the sales call.* It's important in any business plan to set goals and measure progress from making sales calls. Figure 7.6, a grid for tallying the total number of sales calls you make in each target market, provides an efficient way to keep track of these sales calls over time.

Figure 7.4

Create Business-Producing Tactics for Your Target Market

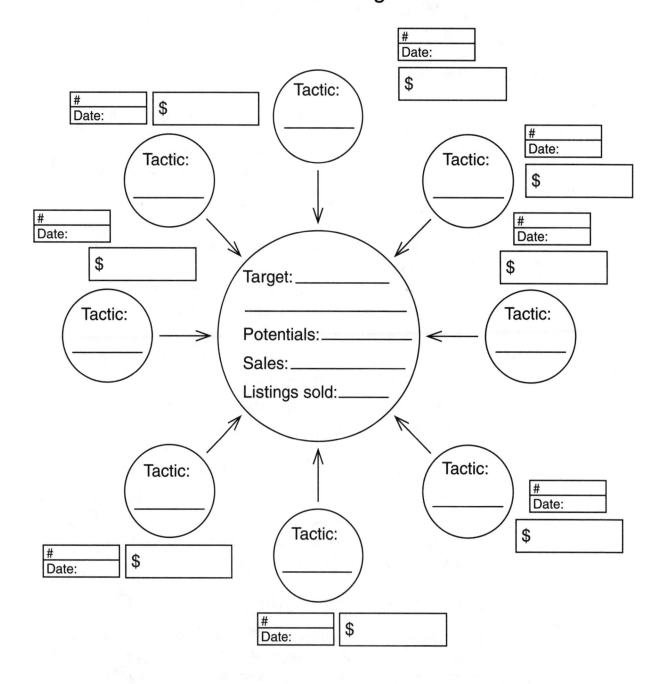

Total tactical impact (number of in-person/telephone): _____ (transfer to Figure 6.6.)

Total budget for this market: $ _____ . Add this budget to your total marketing budget.

Figure 7.5

Itemization of Tactics with Dates, Budget

Name your target market. Put your tactics in order of the dates to be accomplished. Assign work to be accomplished in each tactic. Add your budget figure. Then, tally your total budget from this target market. Put the total budget on your marketing budget worksheet.

Target Market: _____

Tactic*	Assigned To	To Be Done By	Budget

*Use tactical planning worksheet to create mini-plan for each of your tactics, if needed.

Figire 7.6

Total Sales Calls* Projected for Each Target Market (Prospecting)

Month: G = Goal A = Actual	Jan		Feb		Mar		Apr		May		Jun		Jul		Aug		Sep		Oct		Nov		Dec		Totals
	G	A	G	A	G	A	G	A	G	A	G	A	G	A	G	A	G	A	G	A	G	A	G	A	
Target Market																									
Past clients/customers																									
Sphere of influence																									
Geographical farm																									
For-sale-by-owners																									
Expired listings																									
Targeting businesses																									
Other																									

Grand Total – Prospecting

* In person or telephone

Developing Your Tactics

Simply putting a tactical idea in a circle may not provide enough information for you to take action on the idea. The worksheet in Figure 7.7 will help you fully develop your tactical idea. Here's how this worksheet can work for you. Let's say you decide to create a series of three mailers for the year that you want to send to your geographical farm. However, first you must create them. There are several steps to consider when creating a mailer:

- Decide on the frequency.

- Decide on the messages.

- Hire a graphic designer (or use company-generated materials).

- Hire a writer, if needed.

- Decide on a printer; meet with printer to decide on paper, color, etc.

- Create dates for completion of each step.

By using the worksheet in Figure 7.7, you can ensure that your creative idea becomes reality.

Must the Idea Be Unique?

Sometimes agents worry about whether a particular tactic is great—if it's not a unique idea, it shouldn't even be considered! That attitude can surely get in the way of tactical implementation!

Recently, in a personalized marketing class that I was teaching, groups of agents were brainstorming ideas that had worked. One group was fortunate to have Wendy, a wonderful personal marketer in the Seattle area. Wendy had spent thousands of dollars buying materials, attending high-level seminars and experimenting with various personalized marketing techniques. Ruth, an agent in this group kept critiquing Wendy's million-dollar suggestions. Finally, I took the "master critiquer" aside. I told her that, in order for Wendy to share any more valuable ideas, within the next month Ruth would have to try one of the next five ideas presented. In other words, I asked her to change her game. Until she resigned the job of "group evaluator," Ruth could not recognize the value of Wendy's ideas, could not translate others' ideas to her situation, could not grasp or implement them.

Here's the danger of letting the Ruths of the world stay in the critique mode: People like Ruth can steal your dreams, put a damper on your ability to create, annihilate your enthusiasm. Don't let them. Rather than think in terms of the *best tactic ever created*, simply look back over all the marketing tactics you have noticed in any business. You will remember many wonderful tactics that you can translate to your real estate world.

Figure 7.7

Tactical Development

Each tactic needs to be developed properly to ensure its cost-effectiveness. Use this worksheet to create each tactic.

Target market: _____

Tactic: _____

Number of contacts planned with this method: _____

Any dialogue or script needed: _____

_____

_____

Recommended dialogue: _____

_____

_____

_____

_____

Any written materials needed: _____

_____

Outline for written materials: _____

_____

_____

_____

_____

_____

Who will do the preparation work? _____

When is work to be completed? _____

Budget: _____

Notes: _____

_____

Getting ideas isn't really a problem. Having the confidence to translate them, to develop them, to put them to work is the real challenge.

Keeping Track of Your Tactics

The next few grids (Figures 7.8 through 7.11) will help you to wisely spend your money. These grids can be used by real estate companies to create and measure the effectiveness of their marketing plans, too. To get the most out of your business planning process, involve your manager. Ask to be included in some aspect of your office's planning process, so you can use your office's market research and tap into its marketing moves (more about that in Chapter 8).

What Do You Want from Your Promotions?

To measure results, first decide what you want from your promotions. Do you want the reader to be so motivated that he or she will pick up the phone and call the agent? That type of objective, called *merchandise*, is one of two advertising objectives (the other is institutional, which is discussed later in this chapter). Merchandise type of advertising is used when you want a response from the consumer *now*. Commonly, print advertising is used to reach your merchandise objectives; sometimes radio or television advertising is used. For example, put an ad about a home in the paper and write the ad so that it will take the caller through the four buying steps, ending with the desired outcome—action to call you:

1. Get their *attention*—with a snappy headline.
2. Grab their *interest*—with compelling copy.
3. Create *desire*—with emotional "hooks."
4. *Close*—to motivate the reader to call us.

It makes sense that, to measure the effectiveness of that kind of advertising, you would measure the number of phone calls that resulted from placing your ad. Figure 7.8 provides a grid for measuring the results of your media tactics that have a *merchandise* objective.

Measuring More than Just Calls

When I was a new agent, I worked for a small company. The company placed ads in the newspaper about low-priced homes. The homes invariably sounded better than they looked. But those ads generated a lot of calls from buyers who needed to buy a low-priced home. However, it was hard to qualify the buyers. Then, when I showed them the home they called

Figure 7.8

Media Sources of Business

Use this to keep track of your media placements and to make adjustments in your plan.

Date	Agent	Property Owner's Name and Address	Sign Call	General Info	"Block Ad"	"Scatter" Ad	Walk-In	Appointment	Comments / Other

about, they were invariably disappointed. So, although I got many calls from our ads, I got relatively few qualified buyers, and even fewer sales. What I did get were people who felt they had been tricked by clever ad writing.

Establishing high levels of trust and confidence with buyers and sellers is one of the most difficult things to accomplish. In the past, some advertising schemes have enticed people to call real estate companies. But because of the way the ads were written, agents had to overcome bait-and-switch tactics, which created low levels of trust and confidence. If you want to create a strong career, don't resort to bait-and-switch tactics. Having a merchandise goal of *sales made* instead of just calls generated takes you from the perception of "sleazy salesperson" to sales consultant. The grid in Figure 7.9 will help you compare the results of your media sources of business. When we used this grid in our office to compare our results in three newspapers, we discovered that our local newspaper ad cost us $900 to get a call that resulted in a sale!

An office may retain on average $1,200 per sale. Obviously, spending three-quarters of that amount to generate the call that led to the sale is not a prudent business decision. When managers and agents share their market research on advertising vehicles, everyone can take advantage of that information and invest their dollars wisely.

Back to an earlier statement: Before you can measure the results of your advertising, you must determine whether the objective is merchandise or institutional. If you plan to measure the success of your advertising by calls, appointments and sales, be sure that your goal is a *merchandise* one—that you expect the phone to ring as a result of your advertising.

Few agents understand the principles of merchandise or *direct response* advertising. If you want to create effective direct response mail pieces (or any kind of merchandise advertising), read the books listed in the Reference section to see the differences between merchandise and institutional advertising and how to pick the appropriate advertising objective.

Advertising To Enhance Your Image

Why does Nike advertise using no shoes, no prices and no direct reference to Nike shoes? Without this information, how does Nike expect the phone to ring? Do they expect the consumer to read the ad, drop everything and march into the athletic shoe store to purchase a particular pair of Nikes? No, they don't. With this advertising campaign Nike does not have a *merchandise* objective. Instead, Nike wants consumers to relate in their minds an attractive, contemporary active quality of life with Nike shoes. If we purchase Nike shoes, we will have that quality of life. This kind of image-enhancing objective is called *institutional* advertising.

Figure 7.9

Cost per Medium

Tally the results of your media sources of business. Use this worksheet to compute the cost of each medium to:

(1) generate a call
(2) generate a lead
(3) generate a sales or listing sold

Adjust your media dollars to get a "bigger bang for your buck."

Medium	Cost per Ad	Cost per Lead	Cost per Listing Sold/Sale	Analysis

Advertising with an institutional objective is subtle and long-term-results-oriented; it requires a lot of thought and creativity to implement successfully. Image-enhancing advertising starts with the creation of one powerful theme, and all promotional efforts about that service or product tie into that theme over time. In Chapter 8 we will discuss overall personal marketing themes, along with some personal marketing guidelines.

Marketing Promotions in the '90s

Looking at the advertising of past decades will give you a sense of advertising trends. With a bit of research, you can discover how the internationally famous marketing gurus are guiding the marketing of products and services today. Watch television ads, and read magazine and newspaper ads. Study the ads, and ask yourself:

- Does the ad talk about the features of the product or service directly?
- Does the ad tell the benefits of the product or service?
- Does the ad speak directly about the product or service in any fashion?
- Does the ad have an overall theme? What is it?
- Would you say the ad has a lifestyle theme?
- What market does this ad speak to?
- What markets does this ad not appeal to?
- What is the ad's objective?
- Is the ad's objective merchandise or institutional?

You will find that lifestyle, or image-enhancing advertising, is dominant today. This type of advertising does not ask consumers to make an immediate move. Rather it slowly teaches them to associate that product or service with their *most pleasant, successful view of themselves.* To become most successful, consumers will buy that particular product or service.

Measuring the Results of Institutional Advertising

If the objective of the institutional advertising isn't to make the phone ring, how can the effect of this advertising be measured? A few years ago, when I worked for one of the largest U.S. real estate companies, I was on a task force to create a marketing plan. We hired an independent survey firm to do market research to find out what the public thought about our company—its perceived image. We also wanted to find out what consumers thought about our competition. Armed with that information, we could build on our strengths, shore up our weaknesses, while keeping in mind our public's perception of our competition.

Through asking these types of questions of hundreds of consumers, the research firm found out that our company was rated first in customer satisfaction—at 8.1 on a scale of 1 to 10. Our nearest competitor was rated 7.9. That was our benchmark. We set a goal that our customer satisfaction rating would become 9.5 as a result of our marketing efforts. We made a comprehensive marketing plan to communicate, measure and refine our customer relationships, so that we could increase our valued image in the community. At that point, I left the company, so I don't know the end results. But to complete this cycle, a company would implement a one-year image campaign and measure the results of the campaign via another public survey. With the positive results, the company could promote this success.

You and Institutional Advertising

How do you, an individual, translate this *institutional* objective to your own promotional challenges? First, ask yourself what your advertising is for. Do you expect the phone to ring as a result of your advertising? Or do you have a long-term objective, such as Nike's?

What do you want the consumer to do as a result of your advertising—pick up the phone, or attach a message of real estate success with *you* in the mind of that consumer? Decide first, before you create your advertising pieces. The trend is away from direct response advertising (for either products or services) and toward image-enhancing advertising (more about this in Chapter 8).

Who Should Spend Money on Image Advertising?

According to the top agents around the country, the best marketing dollars are spent in promoting real estate images—not in advertising homes to get phone calls. So you might conclude that you should buy a huge ad in a newspaper and tout your professionalism. However, it's not quite that simple. Here's the guideline:

Spend money on advertising promotions that reach people who already know of you. For superstars, that means that they can advertise in wider-reaching mediums and *still* reach people who know them—or know of them. For newer agents, it's a different story. Here's an example of a superstar and a new agent grappling with the question of spending institutional dollars. As usual in my office, we started creating our next-year's business plans and meeting together in December. One of my first meetings was with Anne, a 35-year real estate veteran in our office. Anne had lived in our area for most of her adult life. She had created a dynamic, stable real estate career and, in my opinion, was the epitome of the successful real estate agent. Her customers and clients loved her; other agents looked up to her. In all her real estate transactions, she was aboveboard and fair. For the past two years, Anne had spent approximately $1,200 a year advertising monthly in our local newspaper. Her ad looked like a newspaper column—with her photo and an "article" about real estate. Anne did not write the article but paid a service to write it (the service fee was included in the cost of the ad). The article brought Anne the results she was looking for. As she saw the thousands of residents she knew or that knew of her, she received hundreds of comments per year, such as, "Anne, I always read your article in the newspaper." In Anne's opinion, the article perpetuated her image as a local real estate expert. Anne was not looking for a merchandise result, so she was not disappointed when she did not get a phone call every time her picture appeared in the newspaper. For Anne, this expense and vehicle were appropriate.

However, another agent in our office, Mark, was also spending the same amount of money in this paper, rotating his "article" with Anne's. Mark had lived in the area for eight years and had been in real estate one year. His business was growing well, but it would be many years before he would be as well known as Anne. Mark was not spending much money on his circle of influence because the bulk of his money was going to the newspaper ad. To get the biggest "bang for his buck," Mark switched his marketing efforts and dollars to his best source of business—his past customers and clients and circle of influence. Mark got a much better return on that investment.

In the next chapter, we will discuss much more about your personalized marketing choices. For your reference, there is a list of marketing books for your use in the Reference section. One book, *The Managers Guide to Real Estate Marketing*, is especially helpful because it's specifically about real estate marketing.

A Measurement Grid To Keep Costs Down and Profits Up

The worksheet in Figure 7.10 provides a way for you to plan your promotion and to project the desired return on your promotional investment. You can use this grid to project any sort of single promotion or marketing campaign. After you have set up your projected return, you can keep track of your actual return. In addition, by using the categories in Figure 7.10, you can project and measure cost and return on appointments and sales and listings sold (for merchandise objective-based promotions).

Figure 7.10

Promotion Evaluation

Use this sheet to plan and measure the effect of a promotion (tactic) to a specific market.

Promotion description: _____

_____

To what target market: _____

**For what results (increase image or get leads): _____

_____

If to get leads, goals of this promotion: _____

Budget: _____

Time frame: _____

Projected return on investment: _____

_____

Months	1	2	3	4	5	6	Total
Cost/Month							
Projected # of contacts/month							
Projected return/sales							
Actual return							

Analysis: _____

_____

_____

_____

Figure 7.11

Comparison Analysis: Return on Investment

Target Market or Promotion	Time Frame	Total Dollars Spent	Leads Generated	Listings/ Sales	Commissions	Cost per Transaction (# units closed ÷ $ spent)	Evaluation

Comparing One Promotion with Another

Figure 7.11 is one of the most important grids for you to use to save money and decide where to reallocate your dollars. As a professional, you realize that you can't spend money on everything. And you should not spend money on promotions just because someone else is spending money that way. However, it's hard to say "no" when a seller you represent insists you advertise his property—again. It's hard to say "no" when your agent friends spend thousands of dollars advertising themselves in various mailers. How do you know what to say "yes" to? It all has to do with return on investment.

Poor reasons to spend your money are:

• The seller expects it of you.

• Your friends are spending money that way.

Good reasons to spend money are:

• The money will increase your image in your best target markets.

• The money will bring you a certain amount of merchandise return on your investment (phone calls, appointments, listings, sales).

When I first started managing my second office, I asked each agent to prepare a business plan. I found that one agent was spending $300 per month on advertising to strangers—and had received only three phone calls (and no resulting sales or listings sold) that entire year as a result! I asked the agent if he felt the advertising had increased his image as a successful agent in the community? He replied that he hadn't written his advertising to do that; he expected phone calls. Should he continue spending $3,600 for no merchandise return? Should he change his messages to create an overall image-marketing strategy? Should he drop the advertising altogether?

To answer these questions, the agent and I first analyzed the other areas where he was spending money. We started with his best source of business—his past customers and clients. He had been in the real estate business in that area (as well as having grown up there) for three years. He had been reasonably successful and had a large group of acquaintances that he could market himself to. However, he was spending no money in that area. We reallocated his marketing dollars to spend that $300 per month on his circle of influence. We created a campaign around his desired real estate image (more about this in Chapter 8). The result: A business increase of 20 percent over the previous year, including a more valued image in the community as a real estate expert. A bonus: He is doing business with people he knows at a high level of trust and confidence, and he finds his

Figure 7.12

Comparison Analysis: Return on Investment

Target Market or Promotion	Time Frame	Total Dollars Spent	Leads Generated	Listings/ Sales	Commissions	Cost per Transaction (# units closed ÷ $ spent)	Evaluation
Newsletters	1 year	$1,000	4	2	$4,000	$250	Effective
Mailers	1 year	$2,000	6	1	$2,000	$2,000	Not worth cost
Newspaper Advertising	1 block ad	$5,000	0	0	0	—	Didn't meet merchandise objective

business more pleasant. Figure 7.11 provides a means for comparing promotions as returns on your investment. Figure 7.12 shows some comparisons of promotions to illustrate how this grid will work for you.

Summary

In this chapter, you concentrated on the promotional part of your action plan—the specific actions you decide to carry out to increase your business next year. These marketing actions have one of two objectives: *merchandise* or *institutional*. As you can imagine, it's difficult to expect any promotional campaign to have more than one objective, and it makes it very hard to create a campaign if both objectives are expected. You learned the importance of maintaining the marketing relationships between target market, tactics and you. You have several tools for setting and measuring marketing objectives. In the next chapter, we will investigate how to create an overall marketing strategy that will increase dramatically the effectiveness of your marketing plan.

How To Market *You*

"By reviewing my business and building on my personal strengths, I found that I could do what I loved and have it work for me in my business life."

—Gail H. Gores

In This Chapter ·····················

Creating *you*

Positioning *you*

Secrets to personalized marketing success

Personalized marketing choices for your career stage

From *bombast* to *quality*

What Is Personalized Marketing?

As real estate licensees, we have a habit of tossing around words without good explanations. The habit must come from our fascination with stories and actions. Because we want to get to the good parts—the activities and stories about what we do—we don't take the time to define our terms *before* we launch into examples and advice.

To avoid misunderstandings, first consider the definition of personalized marketing: *The activity of promoting oneself to identified target markets, with the objective of increasing one's image and credibility to those markets.*

119

The following is an example of personalized marketing: Scott, an agent in our office, sent an oversize postcard, showing his listing-to-sold-listing success record, to former customers and clients. He promoted himself to an *identified target market*, giving his customers the messages he wanted them to know about him. His objective was to create credibility and increase his image as a real estate professional to that market. The card closes with a "call to action."

Note that Scott's card was created to hit a particular target market. One of the mistakes that agents make in attempting to market themselves is that they don't work *from the market to the tactic.* That is, they create a card but don't know what it's for—or who to send it to.

The definition of personalized marketing provides two important principles:

1. *To be effective, all personalized marketing tactics must be related to a particular target market.* Think of it this way. These promotional tactics are created to speak personally to a particular market when you can't be there. All the personalized marketing moves that agents make are *tactics,* which must be related to a particular market to be effective.

2. *The objective of personalized marketing should be mainly institutional.* Although Scott asked for a call, he will not be disappointed if he does not get one. Why? His main objective with the postcard was an institutional one: He wanted to increase his image and credibility with one of his best target markets. He wanted to remind his customers of his superior sales record so that they would know what to say about him to others.

Creating *You*

In the "vision" section of this book (see Chapter 4), you laid some groundwork for your personalized marketing efforts. You focused on your vision of you as a successful real estate professional, identified your specialties and your target markets, and outlined the specific services you provide. You have been thinking about the *added values* you can provide to a customer or client. Now you can decide on a marketing theme—a simple statement or thought that captures your essence and promotes that essence to your desired target markets.

Notice that I did not say *slogan.* Why? Slogans consist of a few words that capture your essence. Slogans sound as though they would solve the "theme" problem. Unfortunately, writing slogans is really tricky. Internationally famous ad agencies spend hundreds of thousands of their clients' dollars trying to come up with memorable slogans for their products and services. Agencies dedicate their best creative minds to the task. Then the companies who hire these agencies spend millions of dollars trying to get consumers to relate the slogan to the product. What happens? Only a few slogans become memorable—even at a cost of millions of marketing dollars and the work of the best creative minds in the business.

Here's an example. What's Nike's slogan? *Just do it.* What's Reebok's? Only one out of twenty people I ask can answer that question, even though Reebok spent the same millions of dollars trying to get us to remember *Life is short. Play hard.* Why do you remember Nike's slogan but not Reebok's? Is Nike's a better slogan? Were they first with a sports slogan? Is Nike a better shoe? Your guess is as good as mine. But the point is that a good slogan is difficult to come up with. Then, after you've created the slogan, you must allocate thousands of your marketing dollars to teach your consumers to attach that slogan to your product.

Slogans are meant to strike an emotional chord that relates our hearts and head, while attaching that feeling to the product. That's complex. Notice that I have discussed only *product* slogans. But you are a personal service. That's even harder. How can you distill the essence of your personal service to a few words that capture the best *you*? Can you think of a service slogan that is memorable—in any business?

Slogans—The '90s Version

Does Nike's slogan tell you anything about Nike's products? Or does it suggest something about *lifestyle*? Think of some advertising slogans of the past:

Winston tastes good like a cigarette should.

Pepsi-Cola hits the spot. Twelve full ounces, that's a lot.

Camay, the soap of beautiful women.

In the past, slogans sold us on the attributes of the product. Today, slogans suggest that, if we use the product advertised, we will have the kind of lifestyle we want. You, the agent, are a bundle of complex emotions, thoughts and background. Your "bundle" creates the unique mix of personal services that you provide to a buyer or seller. Don't try to capture that bundle in a slogan. Instead, develop marketing *themes* and variations. Otherwise, you will sound like Betty (see Chapter 7), who wanted to advertise herself to lots of strangers, using a slogan. As Betty, many agents pick slogans that seem to guarantee certain levels of personal service. That is dangerous because this type of slogan will set up expectations that you may not be able to meet. *Expect Excellence* is a slogan that a large bank in our area uses. Unfortunately, many of its present (and past) customers have gotten poor service. Now the joke is: When you bank with this bank, *don't* expect excellence! According to a marketing saying, "the customer doesn't know what he's getting—until he doesn't." Slogans can set up unrealistic expectations in the minds of consumers.

What You Want Your Target Markets To Remember

Above all, you want people to remember your name.

Select a graphic artist to create a memorable *signature*. It becomes your *logo*. Don't have a separate logo and slogan. Your company has a signature, perhaps a logo, and a slogan. If you create all those on top of what your company provides, you will confuse the public. According to national marketing surveys, the public can only read *six* words on a line—on a billboard. How do you expect your target markets to sort out your name, your logo, your slogan, your message, your company name, your company logo, your company slogan, your designations and your phone numbers— all on a postcard? Create a *signature* and promote your overall marketing strategy.

If you are confused by this advice, *test market* these principles. Look at the junk mail that you received at home. Study the pieces that you would open. What is memorable about them? Are they clean and clear, or are they cluttered and wordy? The public will look at your marketing pieces exactly like you look at your junk mail.

Developing Themes To Get Your Name Out

What does the public think about real estate agents? In a customer satisfaction survey by *Consumer Reports*, the public rated real estate agents 10 percent lower in customer satisfaction than other businesses rated. How do real estate agents increase their customer satisfaction levels with consumers? Do they brag that they're "number one in service," say that they're professional, or provide slogans that promise excellence? To a public that has already rated real estate agents low in customer satisfaction levels, these slogans are unbelievable. They would not change the perceived value of the service.

Today, to develop effective marketing pieces, you must *market our records of success*: What you did, not what you promise to be like. Scott's

Figure 8.1

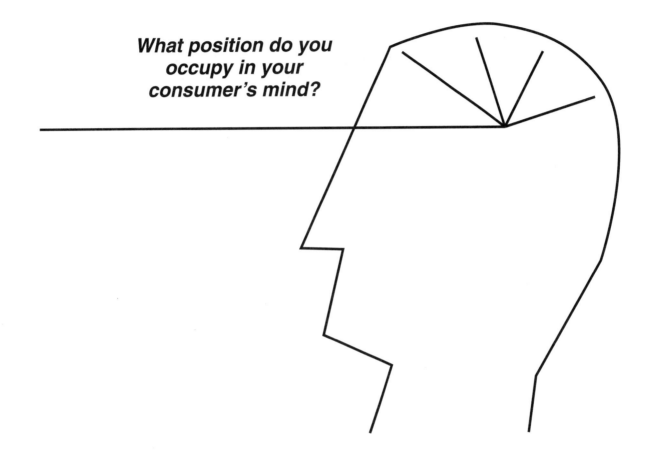

marketing postcard is a good example of *promoting success.* When Scott started working in our office, he set standards of performance for himself. (You can do this by following the guidelines in this book). He decided he wanted 100 percent of his listings to sell in less than average market time. To create that kind of a sales record, Scott developed qualifying, listing and marketing strategies. As you can imagine, Scott never did a listing presentation for an unqualified seller. He would not list an overpriced home. His sales strategy gave Scott several advantages, one of which is time management. He did not waste time with homes and sellers that would not enhance his listing record. After all, Scott had his reputation to consider. Scott realized at the beginning of his career that he wanted to promote his *success.* From being in the contracting business, Scott knew that people believed what he *did,* not what he promised to *do.*

To develop your theme, set standards of performance for yourself. Create strategies to attain those standards of performance. Then use those proofs of success to promote yourself. With a theme of *sold listings*, Scott targeted serious sellers. As Scott evolved in his career, he developed variations of this theme. He created cleverly worded sub-themes to communicate with his target markets. He caught his target markets' attention by creating intriguing flyers (currently, he uses Madonna and cartoon characters to ask agents to inspect his listings). When Scott promotes a playful image, he enhances his credibility by reminding agents that, in order to sell that property, they had better move fast—since his listings sell quickly. See how a smart theme impacts both your internal (agents) and external (consumer) publics?

Positioning *You*

Themes allow you to do what the marketing world calls *positioning*. According to Al Ries and Jack Trout, the advertising gurus who identified this concept, positioning is *not what you do with a product but what you do to the mind of a prospect*. By developing themes, you teach the prospect to think of you in a certain way. And the strongest positioning occurs when, at the mention of real estate agent, the consumer immediately thinks of you (see Figure 8.1). For example, refer back to the Kleenex® example cited in Chapter 4. For more information on "positioning," read the marketing classic *Positioning: The Battle for Your Mind* by Al Ries and Jack Trout. Hal Kahn has an excellent chapter on real estate positioning in his book, *The Manager's Guide to Real Estate Marketing*. Figure 8.2 provides a questionnaire for you to use in creating some positioning statements. Be aware, though, that you can easily slip into "sloganitis" by carrying positioning to a simplistic level. Don't try to come up with a catchy positioning statement (e.g., When you're ready, call Betty). Instead, capture your unique services and talents and develop themes around them based on your real estate successes. Keep your desired position in your mind, and communicate it to your target markets' minds.

Six Secrets to Personalized Marketing Success

Even though real estate agents like to think they are marketers, they are really *sales* specialists. However, when you *market* yourself, you need to use marketing principles. The following are six marketing principles applied to your personalized marketing challenges.

Figure 8.2

How To Position Yourself

1. Create specific benefit statements based on your background and unique qualities.
   Your unique qualities: _____
   _____
   _____

   How they benefit buyers/sellers: _____
   _____
   _____

   Your background (work, talents, volunteer, family): _____
   _____
   _____
   _____

   How it benefits buyers/sellers: _____
   _____
   _____
   _____

2. Create competitive services to an unowned specific market.
   Target market(s): _____
   _____
   _____

   Your competition in market: _____
   _____
   _____

   Valuable services you can provide to market :_____
   _____
   _____

   Your positioning statement: _____
   _____
   _____
   _____
   _____

1. *Underpromise. Overdeliver.* According to one marketing survey, consumers get 500,000 messages a year asking them to pay attention to a marketer's message. They are so overcommunicated with that they don't even pay attention, even when they should! So that these messages get through these "consumer filters," marketers have resorted to ever bigger "filter crashers"—outlandish tricks, sleazy double entendres, neon colors. One of the most dangerous tactics has been to promise anything to get in the door. Recently, I saw an exposé on a carpet cleaning company that promised to clean carpets for a ridiculously low price. Then, when their cleaners got to the house, they quadrupled the price. That's called *bait and switch*. With strategies like that, it's no wonder that people are wary of salespeople!

   How do you create personalized marketing tactics that crash the filters without promising the moon, the stars and the sky? You don't. You *underpromise and overdeliver.* You are dealing with the largest investment most consumers ever make. Your approach must first establish trust and confidence. Let your messages speak about your past accomplishments. Then you won't fall into the trap of setting expectations so high that you cannot meet the public's expectations.

2. *Make your messages benefits to consumers.* Sally created a resume to use as a personalized marketing piece to her target markets. Her resume stated facts about herself: educational and work background, sales record and designations. Sally had fallen into a common trap—she had created a list of features and assumed that readers could figure out why these features were valuable to purchasers and sellers. Don't stop at the features. Create *benefits* of these features that are perceived as valuable to particular customers and clients. As you write your personalized marketing pieces, think like a consumer. Imagine your reader with a question: "What's in it for me?" (see Figure 8.3). If you aren't familiar with this process, the following technique (I call it "consumer think") can help you:

   When I (the consumer) use_____

   I will get_____.

   For example, from a buyer's perspective: "When I take part in the special counseling session that Carla Cross offers, I will be assured that I will be able to purchase the homes I will be shown." Using the strategy above will help you design consumer-targeted programs with benefits—benefits especially valuable to the people whose attention and interest you want to capture.

Figure 8.3

Your Consumer

"What's in it for me?"

3. *Use outside-in thinking.* Figure 8.4. illustrates what happens when you try to guess what the customer wants. Turn the process around: Instead of making choices for your customers, ask them. Think "outside-in." Thuan, a top agent with a northwest company, decided to create a brochure. She studied other agents' brochures and sketched a rough draft of her ideas. She showed the draft to her consumers and clients and asked them if they thought the theme and

Figure 8.4

Inside-Out Thinking

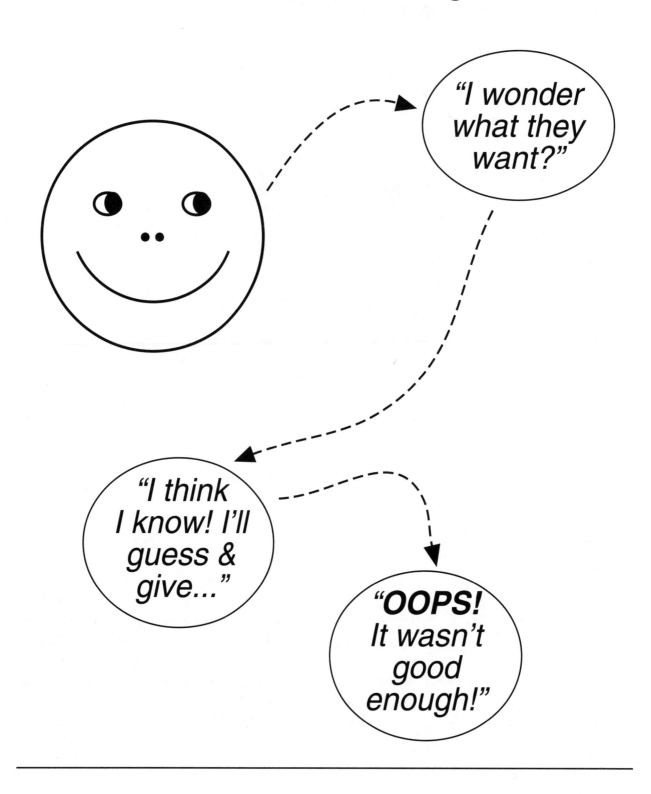

information in the brochure really represented how they thought of her. She got valuable feedback, applied it to her message and created a highly individual brochure that truly represented Thuan. To close the marketing loop, she sent brochures to all the customers and clients who assisted her, thanking them for their efforts. And Thuan asked her "marketing consultants" to assist her in referrals by distributing her brochure.

Here's another idea from a top agent: When you close the sale, ask buyers or sellers to jot down the two words that they think best describe your service. Ask them to note which of your services was most valuable, what services they would like next time, recommendations for additional services. (Use the survey provided in Figure 3.4 to get testimonials and refine your services.) If you like the comments, ask them for permission to include these comments in your personalized marketing communications. You will discover which of your services had great impact, which services that you thought were valuable were of less value to your customer. Very importantly, you will learn how to do better next time.

4. *"Bad advertising is for an audience of one. Good advertising is for an audience of many."*   As you spend your marketing dollars and decide on your tactics, ask yourself whether you are doing some of these tactics just to prove that you have the money or to have other agents say, "Those are great brochures." Recently, I saw a billboard advertising two agents that stated: "the sign of success." I knew the successful agents in that area, yet I had never heard of these agents. Were they overpromising and underdelivering? What was the purpose of the billboard? Since the agents did not have name recognition in that target area, were they expecting the expenditure of several hundred dollars a month to provide them name recognition and credibility? How long would it take for the billboard to change the public's perception of them? Who were the agents targeting? Did they have a distribution plan to support their claims and their billboard cost? For their stage in these agents' careers, their money would have been better spent on other vehicles—ones that would impact their best target markets. Be sure that your advertising isn't ego-driven.

5. *Frequency is more important than reach.*   Two agents called their company's corporate office to find the cost of a one-page ad in the regional newspaper. They were considering placing a full-page ad in the Sunday newspaper at a cost of $10,000 to "get their names out." Since the cost was $10,000, they could place the ad only once!

Figure 8.5

The Power of Consistency

An ad ran in a newspaper once a week for 13 weeks.

After that period:

> 63% remembered ad at the end of 13 weeks
> 32% remembered ad 1 month later
> 21% remembered ad 6 weeks later

Retention drops quickly when advertising stops.

Frequency and consistency, not the cleverness of the message, are the big determinants of effective advertising.

Luckily, the corporate office was able to convince them of their folly. Would you "turn yourself in" to a real estate agent that had advertised once in your Sunday newspaper? Would you remember the name after having seen it once? Of course not. *Frequency is more important than reach* because, to get your name inside the consumer's head, you must repeat it again and again. Direct mail studies show that consumers throw out mail messages *seven times* before they even read one. They read it three times before they take action. That's *twenty-one* times to the same reader to expect action! Instead of spending $10,000 on a one-time ad to reach strangers, spend $2,000 communicating with 300 past customers and clients 12 times during the year. You will get a much greater return on your investment.

6. *A consistent message ensures that consumers remember you.* This principle goes right along with frequency and reach. To get your name firmly imbedded in consumers' minds, deliver a consistent message *over time.* How much time?

☞   Marketers suggest *no less than one year* for any advertising campaign. As you design your marketing messages to your target markets, commit to at least one year of consistent, frequent messages. Too often, marketers stop because they don't see an immediate return. Ironically, they stop just before they could expect to see results! As part of my personal marketing program as a speaker, I have written numerous articles over the past six years in various real estate publications. I began wondering about whether those articles were worth my time and efforts. In my sixth year, I started getting comments: "We see your name everywhere." "You are certainly the expert on that." My advice is: About the time you are ready to give up on the futility of your image campaign, extend it three months. Then stop, look and listen. People will tell you what wonderful things they have heard about you! It takes time—consistency and frequency. Figure 8.5 provides some statistics on consistency and retention. It shows the retention results on an ad that ran once a week for 13 weeks. Have long-term faith in the power of consistent and frequent messages to identified target markets.

Leverage Your Company's Materials

Last year, a company invited me to conduct a workshop on personalized marketing. In preparing for the workshop, I asked the owner about the materials available. The company (a member of a national franchise) had dozens of beautifully produced materials available for agents' use. I was impressed by the quality and consistency of the materials. However, both the owner and the agents indicated that the agents were not using any company materials. This is common—few agents use company-created materials because they think they must design their own unique materials. When they investigate design and implementation, they find the process costly and time-consuming. Or they design one humongous newsletter, send it out once, and that's it.

☞   What's the answer? *Buy your company materials and customize them.* One agent creates stickers that look like business cards. He sends out company-generated materials and just adds his sticker. Another agent sends out the company newsletter, along with a personalized-stationery insert. Don't try to reinvent the wheel, especially in the early years of your career. Companies spend hundreds of thousands of dollars in marketing costs and hundreds of hours of creative experts' time creating sophisticated marketing pieces—materials that capture the company's quality image. Take advantage of your company's design money and the ad agencies' expertise that produce quality materials. As I travel around the country

Figure 8.6

Brochures

Answer these questions:

1.   What's it to accomplish for you?

2.   Is it part of a campaign? Where does it fit in your program?

3.   Who will get it? What are they interested in?

4.   What's the format (e.g., size, print, photos)?

5.   How will it be distributed (e.g., mail, handout, letter)?

6.   How can you get extra mileage (e.g., publication, news release, speech)?

Creating Your Brochure

1.   Identify your audience.

2.   Decide on overall marketing strategy—a theme.

3.   Follow the sales steps—**AIDA (Attention, Interest, Desire, Action)**.

4.   Use bold graphics.

5.   Use colors—full color is more effective.

6.   Use texture.

7.   Be consistent.

8.   Build trust:
     - Testimonials
     - Underpromise, overdeliver
     - Years in business—benefits of community service

9.   Use effective headline.

10. Use few words. Use bullets.

speaking, I see thousands of examples of agents' marketing materials—few are wonderful. Agents are *salespeople,* not marketers, ad agencies, writers or graphic artists. Instead of creating an inferior representation of *you,* start with your company materials and learn from them. Remember to figure your *time* as a variable when you consider creating your own materials. And ask yourself: *what is this for?* Do you read all the newsletters you get from all sources? Do you critique every article and word? No, of course not. Neither do your customers read and critique every article and word of *your* newsletters. Normally, they look at it, smile when they see your name and/or picture, glance over the newsletter and toss it.

A word to the growth-oriented, experienced agent: After you have used the materials and distribution systems provided by your company, you can progress into a marketing phase where you develop your own marketing pieces. To make that move, select a good ad agency, or find a graphic artist, writer, desktop publisher and printer. Dave Beson's book, *Personal Promotion*, offers hundreds of helpful hints about the production of promotional pieces.

Brochures, Newsletters and Direct Mail

Agents go through phases with their personalized marketing efforts. For a while, the vogue was to create a personal *brochure. Everyone* rushed to create a brochure. But, because the agents didn't know the basics about brochure design and use, many were poorly written or not distributed for good effect. Figure 8.6 provides a checklist to use in designing an effective brochure. The questionnaire in Figure 8.7 helps you create focus for your brochure. The challenge with brochures is: Brochures are relatively expensive. Therefore, to be cost-effective, they must be ordered in large quantities. But, as you establish and grow your career, your business focus changes. It is better to start with a feature-benefit one-page sheet with your picture. Begin by using company stationery to keep your costs down. (Your company will probably ask you to purchase stationery for this purpose.) Put your copy on a word processor and change it as needed. After using this format for a year, you can decide whether you need a brochure and how to create one that avoids frequent changes.

Figure 8.8 provides tips on *newsletters.* I do not recommend producing a newsletter until you are in high growth as an agent. It takes writing, organizing and producing skills to create a newsletter that competes in "look" with those produced by newsletter companies. Sell real estate, and let others create printed materials!

Figure 8.7

Questionnaire: For Your Brochure

Specialties

Price ranges, customer/client groups you specialize in: _____
_____
_____

How you help these markets solve their problems: _____
_____
_____

Qualities

Work/volunteer/personal background: _____
_____

Traits and skills you bring to real estate: _____
_____

How these can benefit buyers/sellers: _____
_____

Experience

Length of time in real estate: _____
_____

How this benefits buyers/sellers: _____
_____

Education

Education and designations: _____
_____

Value to buyers/sellers: _____
_____

Achievements

Achievements: _____
_____

Value to buyers/sellers: _____
_____

Quotes

What buyers/sellers say about you: _____
_____

Possible testimonials: _____
_____

Figure 8.8

Newsletters

1. Use format of two pages or more.

2. Use black ink on colored paper.

3. Use black ink plus another accent color on white paper.

4. Full-color photos—large mass of primary color.
   - Don't use pastels.
   - Be careful of skin tones.
   - Mix color and black-and-white.

5. Be sure it's clean and clear.

6. Make it consistent with the image of your company.

7. Make it consistent with your vision, position, overall marketing strategy.

8. Identify your audience. Speak directly to them.

9. Don't write more than they'll read.

10. Use as part of your distribution plan to your target markets over time.

Materials such as newsletters and brochures are tactics for communicating with your target markets. One method of communication is *direct mail*. Again, since agents are not generally marketing majors, they need precise information on various types of distribution programs in order to ensure that their marketing tactics are effective. Figure 8.9 provides some tips on direct mail. Before you start with a merchandise objective for direct mail (a response to you), study how direct mail is written.

Figure 8.9

Direct Mail Tips

1. Select the right mailing lists.
    -   Price category
    -   Recent response
    -   Mail offers response

2. Develop your offer. What is it and what response do you want?

3. Make outside envelope writing—teaser statement (prediction).

4. Answer all questions in letter to get a reply.

5. Use subheads/sizes of type.
    -   Identify key paragraphs.
    -   Underline important points/circle.
    -   Use colored ink.

6. Use postscript—restate major benefit.

7. Use a reply card.

8. To increase response, include brochure (major benefit on cover) or newsletter (two pages).

9. Mailing first class and priority-size envelopes: Write classification on front and back.

Personalized Marketing Choices for Your Career Stage

Throughout this chapter, I have provided guidelines for your marketing choices and design. Now, you need to consider your marketing choices as they relate to your career stage. First, *decide which phase of your career you're in*. Figure 8.10 shows the phases of an agent's career: introduction, growth and maturity. After you pinpoint your career stage, think of yourself as a product you want to market. If you are at the entry level stage, design your personalizing marketing program as if you were introducing a new

Figure 8.10

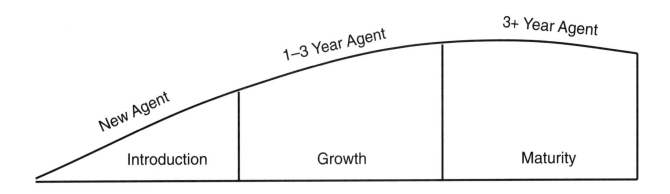

Career Phases

product. If you are at growth, design your program like a product that you want to expand to additional markets. If you are at maturity, design your program to keep that product in the front of the customer's mind. These stages are summarized in Figure 8.11.

Marketing Yourself at Entry Level

You are new, fresh and excited. But, like a new product, you have no success record. Take a tip from successful product marketers. Just as new products are related to successful ones for instant credibility ("New—from the creators of Tide"), create marketing messages that build bridges between your past job, avocation, volunteer or life successes. State them as benefits to customers and clients: "Ozzie's ten years in the restaurant business have given him the perspective on customer satisfaction to make your home dreams come true." Since you have little resources, use non-media or mini-media sources to spread the word. Take advantage of the fact that you have time to meet people face-to-face. While you organize your marketing plan, start your data management program. *Top Producer* is a choice of many agents. (See the Reference section of this book for more information.) If you have a small budget, organize your contacts and run your distribution programs yourself. Consider hiring a high school person to help you. Because you have few or no real estate successes, use your company's successes to give yourself credibility. For instance, the following goal that our office attained is appropriate for agents to use to promote themselves: Our office increased our conversion rates of listings taken to

Figure 8.11

Career Moves by Career Phase

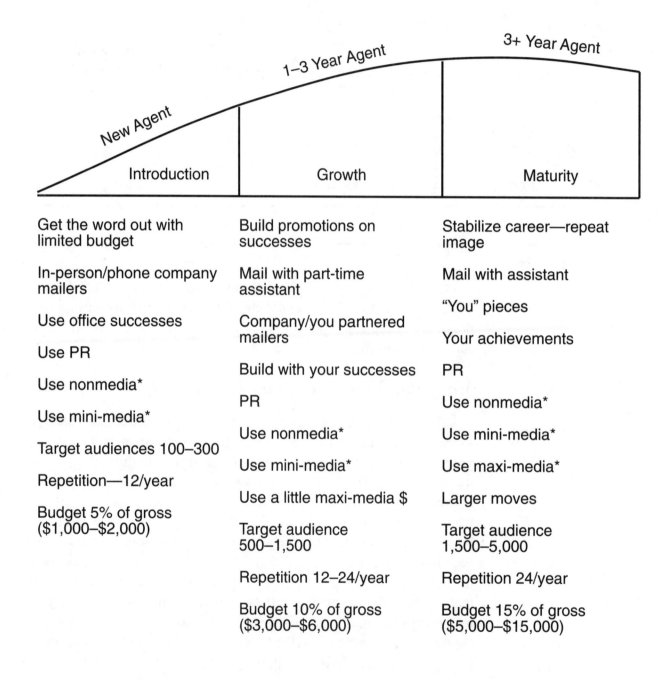

Introduction	Growth	Maturity
Get the word out with limited budget	Build promotions on successes	Stabilize career—repeat image
In-person/phone company mailers	Mail with part-time assistant	Mail with assistant
Use office successes	Company/you partnered mailers	"You" pieces
Use PR	Build with your successes	Your achievements
Use nonmedia*	PR	PR
Use mini-media*	Use nonmedia*	Use nonmedia*
Target audiences 100–300	Use mini-media*	Use mini-media*
Repetition—12/year	Use a little maxi-media $	Use maxi-media*
Budget 5% of gross ($1,000–$2,000)	Target audience 500–1,500	Larger moves
	Repetition 12–24/year	Target audience 1,500–5,000
	Budget 10% of gross ($3,000–$6,000)	Repetition 24/year
		Budget 15% of gross ($5,000–$15,000)

*See Figure 7.1 for promotional choices in these categories.

listings sold by 35 percent in one year! That means we made many more sellers happy, increasing our customer satisfaction levels. See your manager for "good news" that you can use to promote yourself. To save time, money and effort, start with your best source of customers and clients—people you know. Survey them to find out what they think of you as a businessperson. Translate their comments into real estate terms, and start your personalized promotion efforts. Use the company newsletter along with your business card or a business sticker to communicate with your best market. Make your communication plan at least a year long, with 12 communications that year. Include in-person, mail and phone contacts. Reiterate a theme and variations in your communications. And measure your results.

Marketing Yourself at the Growth Stage

You have established a theme. You have communicated with your best markets, using success messages of your office and company. You have kept your costs down and in-person efforts high. Now you're ready to step to the next level: You want to expand your business and be time-efficient.

Because you have at least one target market on your contact management program, you can expand your distribution plan to include other markets. These markets could be geographical areas, business relationships, first-time buyers, etc. To save time, hire a part-time assistant to organize, create and distribute your communications. Because you have a track record of success, promote those successes. Take advantage of free press: "Blow your own horn" each time you attend a real estate course (send these press releases to your target markets with a note telling them you want to keep them apprised of what's happening with your real estate successes). Because you have more marketing money, invest in seasonal gifts to your target markets. Shift from company-oriented messages to you-created messages, keeping in mind that frequency and consistency are more important than reach. Create a brochure to distribute to several of your target markets—your career is now stable enough to give your brochure some "shelf life." Move from in-person and telephone contacts to a steady mail distribution system, interspersing enough personal contacts to keep "high touch" and show people you care.

Marketing Yourself at the Maturity Stage

For some agents, growing their business is very important, even when they have been in business for many years. However, others want to move into the maturity stage of their businesses, where they maintain a steady rate of business. First, let's look at how to grow your business to superstar proportions—a worthy goal after establishing a period of high initial growth. After you have built a multimillion dollar career, your personal base of influence is counted in the thousands. You are known as an area expert, and you are ready for some bigger marketing ideas. Now you need a distribution plan that will keep your name and image in front of those thousands of people. To create and implement a plan of those proportions, hire a full-time assistant. (For more about assistants, see Chapter 9.) Your assistant will create and a run your distribution plan, which will feature your success story. In addition to this concept, here are a few big-idea ways that superstars keep their names in front of their wide public:

- For customers and clients, once a year create a "happening"—a party, a luncheon, a theater event. Promote the event with press releases prior to and after the event.

- Regularly write a newspaper article (paid for) in the local newspaper. Send reprints to all customers and clients, with notes to them, if possible.

- Get yourself featured on superstar panels (local and national). Be included in audiotaped interviews and workshops. Send press releases about these events, along with press releases to your target markets.

- Use audiotapes and videotapes to promote yourself to your customers and clients.

You can see, from these ideas, that the basic marketing principle never changes: Regularly communicate *your real estate successes to people who care*. Exactly how you do this depends on the stage of your career.

Leveling Out Your Business

If you want to level out your business, create a marketing plan that adequately keeps you in touch with your target markets to sustain your level of income. Marketers will tell you that, to keep our levels of income steady, you need to communicate no less than *four times yearly with your most-known market*. Maintainers can use mail contacts and add telephone and in-person contacts to their "most important" list—the 100 to 200 people who give the mature agent the most leads. In Figure 8.12 you will find a list of personal marketing moves by masterminds.

Additional Sources

See Appendix A for sample business plans of agents in a particular stage of their businesses. Use these plans as reference for your own business.

Figure 8.12

Total Marketing Costs and Analysis of % of Gross Income

Transfer your marketing costs for each target market and listing/selling costs to this sheet.

I.   Target Markets to Generate Business

Past customers/clients $ _____

Geographical farm $ _____

Prior profession $ _____

Circle of influence $ _____

Expired listings $ _____

FSBOs $ _____

Other $ _____

Other $ _____

Other $ _____

Total $ _____

II.   Listing Costs (Cost Per Listing x Number of Listings)

Signs/name signs $ _____

Display boxes $ _____

Flyers/brochures $ _____

Print advertising $ _____

Mailings $ _____

Seller gifts $ _____

Other $ _____

Total per listing $ _____

x _____ listings   _____

Total $ _____

III. Other Promotions

Gifts $ _____

Entertainment $ _____

Personal marketing

photos $ _____

brochures $ _____

graphics $ _____

printing $ _____

other $ _____

Business cards $ _____

Sponsorships $ _____

Community service $ _____

Total $ _____

Total Marketing Expenses $ _____

Total Marketing Expense as a % of Income _____ %
(Marketing expense ÷ gross income)

Figure 8.13

Personal Marketing Moves
by Masterminds

Masterminds:

1. Start with people they know—and fully exploit.

2. Define exactly who they want to talk to—the individual (micro-marketing).

3. Talk about benefits to the listener of what the marketer can do for that particular listener.

4. Make a distribution plan—commit to it for one year.

5. Make sure that what the marketer does equals the image of the company and what he/she wants to project.

6. Exploit free publicity.

7. Add services that are valuable to the customer—and promote that service value to the customer.

8. Use targeted print media that speaks to the people who already know of the marketers (church newsletter, dentist's newsletter, club newsletter).

9. Resist maxi-media (no large generic ads in newspapers, etc.)

10. Resist direct mail—unless done right and big bucks are spent consistently.

11. Resist the "big one-shot" (no billboard).

12. Resist slogans, and build themes and variations.

In the Reference section, I have included several books that can help you create effective tactics—books on letters, public relations, etc. Armed with the information here, you have the marketing principles you need to choose confidently the right tactics for you. It will be easy for you to find specific resources for creating the tactics you want (see Figure 8.13).

Back to Your Budget

In Chapter 5, you created your operating budget, estimating your marketing budget. Now you can be more specific. The percent of total marketing dollars to your gross commissions should be between 10 to 20 percent, depending on your years in the business and your marketing goals. Remember: To make money, you must spend money. Figure 8.13 provides the categories needed to create a precise marketing budget.

From *Bombast* to *Quality*

Down-sizing, cocooning, back to basics—they're all economic and social trends of the '90s. The reflections of these trends can be seen in personal marketing, too. In the '80s, the public was bombarded with agent slogans, billboards, full-color print materials, promises—all oversimplifications of an agent's complex bundle of services. Agents bragged that they were "#1 in service" (self-proclaimed!). Today, consumers are better educated. They know how to make choices for expert agent representation. They look past the bragging and promises for believable indicators of past customer satisfaction and quality service. How do you adjust your personal marketing tactics to reflect this greater consumer sophistication? Use the principles in *total quality management* (TQM). TQM is a process of systematic and planned change designed to drive a business toward continuous improvement. It gets the business to focus on who its customers are and what their requirements are, and commits the business to fulfill the customer's requirements with an unrelenting commitment to quality. Applied to the real estate business, this means that agents should continuously improve their service and should emphasize *quality* before all else.

This means, in terms of marketing yourself, that you should switch the emphasis from *bombast* (bragging) toward *quality*. That does not mean that you should brag that you are "#1 in quality"! It means that you should ask the customers what they want, then deliver an even higher quality of service than they expect. The *results* of that quality of service are what you promote:

- Testimonials of satisfied customers and clients
- Results of your consumer surveys
- New consumer services you provide as a result of your surveying and continuous improvement

In TQM, the bottom line is achieved by gathering customers and *keeping them for life.* That is what you want. It saves you promotional dollars and results in a more rewarding, easier-to-administer business.

TQM is the management philosophy that the Japanese embraced after World War II in order to improve the quality—and bottom line—of their products and services. See the Reference section for more information on TQM. By using the principles in this book, you will naturally imbue your business with TQM.

Summary

Personalized marketing efforts are tactics that must be related to specific target markets. Taken out of context (not related to specific markets), personalized marketing efforts are ineffective and costly. There are marketing guidelines (the six secrets to personalized marketing) that real estate marketers can rely on to market themselves. To choose which marketing tactics are appropriate for your career stage, you need to:

- identify your career stage;
- identify your best target markets;
- create tactics that relate to those markets; and
- match your messages of success to your markets, your tactics and your budget.

Armed with the guidelines in this chapter, you can make good business decisions about the marketing parts of your business plan.

CHAPTER

9

Your Professional Development: Plan To Improve

"After 15 years in the real estate business, I have heard it all—or at least most of it. But I continue to need and want information that will improve my business. Looking at my business this way helps me make a difference in my career."

—Vicki Dalisky

In This Chapter ·

Business development/business support

Your overall sales strategy

Raising your performance standards

Support from your manager, office and company

Supporting yourself

Deciding on Priorities

Now that you have designed a marketing plan to increase or maintain your business, you need to consider a plan to support and develop your business. This section of the plan encompasses the following areas:

- Refining your business strategy for increased professionalism
- Increasing your knowledge and skill; association work (professional development)
- Developing systems, materials, business tools and labor to enhance your business (support systems)

145

Figure 9.1

Your Business	
Developing It	**Supporting It**
Sales/Marketing (personal selling) Prospecting Qualifying Listing/Selling Closing Promoting (face-to-face/phone)	Systems Processes Labor Materials Professional Development Courses Associations
Supported By	
Your Marketing Plan	
Your Professional Development/Systems/Plan Support	

Developing and Supporting Your Business

Part of business planning is deciding *who does what*. In this chapter, you will determine some of the duties that you can delegate. To help you make decisions in this portion of the business plan, start by dividing your business into two parts (illustrated in Figure 9.1):

- *Business development*
- *Business support*

Business development includes all the sales activities you do to start, continue and end the sales cycle (see Figure 9.2).

These activities, best portrayed as pure *sales* activities, involve qualifying, counseling, negotiating and closing buyers and sellers. You need to assign yourself to these tasks. You do not want to delegate showing homes, closing buyers or negotiating purchase agreements. However, some activities to support the business cycle can be delegated, which will be discussed later in this chapter.

Increasing Your Sales Effectiveness

Selling and marketing increase the *amount* of business you can do. In addition to increasing the *amount* of your business, you may need to improve your sales skills and information to increase your *effectiveness* in developing your business. You will plan for those increased performance standards in the professional development portion of your business plan. There are systems and processes that you can develop or refine to ensure you raise your performance standards. For instance, if you decide to increase your listing effectiveness to 90 percent listings taken to listings sold, one of the systems you will want to enhance is your marketing presentation. After you have increased your listing effectiveness by developing the parts of the listing process as systems, you can delegate the assembling of these parts to an assistant.

Support for Your Business

What is business support? It's all the activities that *support* sales and marketing:

- Organizing
- Delegating
- Attending meetings
- Following up paperwork
- Writing ads
- Creating marketing pieces
- Writing business plans
- Measuring results
- Previewing
- Attending educational sessions
- Touring office listings

The list could be endless. In fact, some agents make this list their job description! As you analyze your time, *see if you spend too much time in business support* and not enough time in business development. This is a

Figure 9.2

Sales Cycle

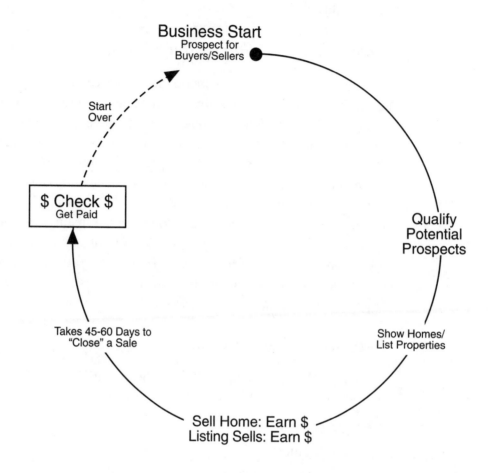

common time management mistake that agents make. If you find your balance is out of kilter, you should create a plan to delegate support duties and refine your systems to get out of the office!

If you need more information and strategies to effectively plan your time, the weekly and daily planning guides in *Up and Running in 30 Days* will get you on track.

Your Basic Business Premise: *Your Overall Sales Strategy*

Now that you have separated your business-developing activities from your business-supporting activities, you can make decisions on how to create a more professional business. First, review the decisions you made in the business planning overview section (with your business objectives). Refer back to Figure 5.13, where you created specific, measurable performance standards to attain in the next year—standards that helped you raise your effectiveness as a pro, standards that are promotable. These priorities formed your *overall sales strategy,* and with this strategy you created your marketing programs. In this chapter, you will decide how to attain your overall sales strategy through professional development, systems and support.

Professional Development: Raising Your Performance Standards

When most new agents attend an initial training program, they are told *not* to list overpriced properties. They all nod their heads in agreement. Then they list any property at any price—because "any listing is better than none." They rationalize that an overpriced listing is acceptable because "the seller may wake up and realize it's overpriced." Unwittingly, these agents create *low performance standards* for themselves. The statistics of the multiple listing service in our area provide evidence that is a common trap: Less than 45 percent of all the homes listed sell within six months—and that's with a healthy real estate market. What does this mean? Agents have settled for low performance standards because:

- they don't possess the sales skills, strategies and systems to list homes properly; and
- they haven't consciously set good standards of performance for *themselves.*

If real estate agents realized that overpricing properties led to high customer dissatisfaction rates and low consumer acceptance, they would not persist in a poor sales strategy. Agents rarely create their own *internal acceptable performance standards.* And, unless they set high standards of performance for themselves, they don't know how to improve their businesses. When agents attend a workshop, they have little reason to apply the information ("it won't work for me in my area"). In other words, if they don't know that they have a problem, they don't look for a solution. Without creating high levels of performance, they have nothing to promote in their marketing plan. Unless they make buyers and sellers happy (a smooth sale, a sold listing), they can't build their personal promotion plan. (I've never seen an agent have the nerve to ask for a referral from a seller whose listing expired!) Success breeds success.

Recently, I was chatting with another manager about an agent who had just joined his company. Although he had admired this agent when the agent had worked for a rival company in the area, he also noted that agent had one bad habit: He overpriced his listings. While the agent was with the rival company, this manager picked up many of these overpriced listings. But the damage had been done to the industry—based on their experience, sellers were disgruntled not only with the former agent, but distrusted all real estate agents. The manager had to choose a very diplomatic but tough agent to deal with these sellers the second time around. And during the business planning session, the manager worked with the agent to set higher standards of listing performance and provided the support the agent needed to change his listing strategy. Today, this agent has new pricing strategies and gets much higher levels of customer satisfaction.

Which areas of performance standards do you want to improve? What business practices are hurting your image and your ability to promote yourself? Figure 9.3 provides checklists for the areas to develop to increase your professionalism. Tie them to your overall sales strategy. Then you will know *why* you are attending that course or joining that organization.

After you develop your new standards, add dates to accomplish these areas. Create a budget for these items. Add your accomplishment dates to your master business calendar. And put your budget totals into your marketing budget.

Systems, Labor, Acquisitions

Working through your marketing plan and reviewing your overall sales strategy will show you if you need additional systems, labor and support to accomplish the objectives in your business plan. Systems include:

- Computer programs
- Computers
- Checklists
- Listing presentations

See Figure 9.4 for a full list of systems. Go through the same process you did with your professional development, assigning dates to accomplish systems refinement and adding budget figures. Put the dates on your master business plan calendar, and add the budget items to your marketing budget.

Additional Labor Needs

Besides mechanical needs and systems, you may need a person to assist you in developing your business. Since many experienced agents consider hiring an assistant, I have provided some planning tools to help you decide whether you need one (see Figure 9.5). Figure 9.6 is a list of tasks that will

Figure 9.3

Professional Development

Date To Accomplish*   **Budget***

Courses, Workshops

_____workshops to develop skill
_____Graduate REALTORS'® Institute (GRI)
_____Certified Residential Specialist (CRS)
_____Certified Real Estate Broker (CRB)
_____REALTORS'® presentations, workshops
_____legal updates
_____technical courses
_____hours toward broker's license
_____hours toward continuing education credit
_____teach real estate course
_____other

Books, Tapes

_____business books bought and read
_____audiotapes purchased
_____videos purchased
_____study programs purchased
_____other

Presentations, Processes, Systems

_____develop listing presentation marketing manual
_____develop buyers' presentation manual
_____develop professional portfolio
_____develop seller qualifying system
_____develop follow-up systems after the sale
_____other

Organizations

_____become more active in REALTOR® organization
_____attend local REALTOR® convention
_____attend National REALTOR® Convention
_____join REALTOR® committee
_____attend company convention
_____other

                                        Total Budget:

Add these dates to your business plan calendar. Put the budget items in your operating or marketing budget.

help you formulate your job description. Be sure to check with your licensing department for the rules and regulations governing assistants' jobs in your state. To create a plan for hiring an assistant, use the tactical planning worksheet in Figure 7.5. For more information on hiring an assistant, see the Reference section.

How To Get Support for Your Business

Recently, I was teaching a basic business planning class. At the break, one of the new agents asked for help with a problem: She had sold several homes and was having trouble with the transactions. She thought her manager was busy and didn't want to intrude. New agents sometimes feel this way because they don't realize the investment that managers have in the success of their careers. I explained that investment—that it included the office's money and my effort. I think of each agent I hire as a developing superstar. It's my responsibility to see that each agent develops a career to his or her desired potential—as quickly as possible. Therefore, I want to help solve any problem an agent may have in creating a great start-up business plan. At the same time, I can teach a new agent the principles of business planning. When managers hire well, they hire with the thought that *each* agent is immensely and singularly important.

Working Proactively with Your Manager

Managers are sometimes regarded as operations people (making floor time schedules, etc.). Some agents think managers exist to solve crises. In my opinion, managers have a more important function—business consulting. Your manager's job description includes office planning, budgeting, staffing, prospecting, closing and training (all of which you do in your business). Your manager has well-developed skills in the same planning process you are involved in. Take advantage of those skills. As you develop your business plan, let your manager be your consultant. A manager's investment in you is tremendous; they want the opportunity to consult with you about your plans for success.

The first step in getting support from your manager is to share your business plan with him or her. Make an appointment, and set aside at least an hour to analyze and explain your plan. Ask your manager to listen to the entire plan and make recommendations. Why? First, you will impress and flatter your manager! (And impressed managers treat agents very well!) Your manager will pay more attention to you. You will gain respect in the office, and you will be brought into activities as a partner in business—which, in truth, you are.

Figure 9.4

Systems/Mechanical/Labor Checklist

Choose from the following areas the systems and support you want to plan for this year.

	*Date To Accomplish**	*Budget**

Mechanical

_____buy a computer, printer
_____buy a typewriter
_____purchase software programs
_____purchase computer hardware
_____take lessons on computers
_____get voicemail, pager
_____purchase car phone
_____purchase fax machine
_____purchase multiple listing service at home
_____other

Labor

_____hire assistant
_____hire mailing service
_____other

Home Office

_____office furniture
_____office supplies
_____fax
_____computer/printer
_____other

Total Budget:

*Put these dates in your business plan calendar. Add these budget items to your operating budget.

Some agents are afraid to involve their managers in the planning process because they are afraid that, if they share their goals and dreams, their managers will hold them to these goals. Remember this: *He or she who makes the plan gets to change the plan!* In my opinion, as long as an agent's business plan meets the *minimum* expectations of our office, how that agent changes the plan monetarily is entirely his or her business.

Figure 9.5

Steps in Hiring an Assistant

Do You Need an Assistant?

1. My business last year:

   listings taken   _____ (units)

   listings sold   _____ (units)

   sales   _____ (units)

2. My goals for the coming year:

   listings taken   _____ (units)

   listings sold   _____ (units)

   sales   _____ (units)

3. Projected assistant salary: _____

   Resources needed:

4. Work I would delegate to an assistant:

5. My reason for wanting an assistant:

6. Office space/considerations:

Other advantages of letting your manager in on your planning process include: Your manager can help you take advantage of office/company plans and programs that can fit right into your business plan and save you money. Two agents in our office were designing their business plan. They wanted to promote themselves to their sphere of influence and debated how to create materials. I suggested that they take advantage of the $70,000 in marketing development and design that our company had spent the previous year in developing agent promotional materials. After reviewing the materials, the agents decided to put that money to work for themselves to save time and effort.

Figure 9.6

Tasks: Assistant Support*

_____ Answer incoming calls and take messages.

_____ Arrange and remind you of appointments.

_____ Compile information for personal income taxes.

_____ Complete follow-up paperwork associated with listings and sales.

_____ Contact sellers and buyers weekly.

_____ Cut out FSBO newspaper ads.

_____ Deliver keys, paperwork, etc.

_____ Do monthly summaries of pending sales, closed sales.

_____ Handle all mail functions, process incoming mail, send bulk mailing, and buy postage.

_____ Schedule and coordinate closings.

_____ Handle incoming calls.

_____ Get feedback on active listings.

_____ Track expireds.

_____ Input MLS listings and changes.

_____ Install or order FOR SALE and SOLD signs.

_____ Keep records of business and personal expenses.

_____ Make and return calls to cooperating salespeople, buyers and sellers.

_____ Order brochures and office supplies.

_____ Prepare and deliver door hangers.

_____ Prepare information for buyers about buying process, current financing sheets, highlight sheets, information for sellers about the listing process, new-neighbor cards and property flyers.

_____ Prepare newsletters or newsletter inserts.

_____ Mail "tell 20" notes.

_____ Mail personalized marketing pieces.

_____ Prepare and keep calendar of all contingency dates, pending sales.

_____ Track FSBOs.

_____ Produce daily account of MLS expired listings.

_____ Research city and county records.

_____ Remind you of special events (birthdays, etc.).

_____ Review closing papers.

_____ Send flowers and gifts.

_____ Send open house thank-yous.

_____ Take dictation and type correspondence and contracts.

_____ Track expenses on rental properties and serve as contact for renters.

_____ Track pending sales and listings.

_____ Send copies of ads to sellers.

_____ Send mail-outs to farm area.

_____ Process all contracts.

* Check the licensing laws of your state to determine which of these tasks can be done only by a licensed assistant.

Your manager can also serve as a valuable resource to the professional development part of your plan. Let's say you need some training skills. Your manager knows the educational training programs offered in the company, in REALTOR® organizations and in the area. Knowing your needs, your manager can arrange training sessions in your office. Take advantage of this resource to save you time and money.

Use the planning worksheet Figure 9.7, to note the support you need from your office and company to reach your business plan objectives.

Supporting Yourself

If you have worked through your plan to this point, you should just about have it all together. Or do you? One of the biggest challenges agents face is to keep going when the going gets tough. I call this *supporting yourself*. What is your plan for support? How do you stay *up* when the business gets you down? Because of the independent and cyclical nature of real estate, I believe all agents need a *self-motivation* plan as part of their business plans. Although this is not part of any business plan I have ever seen, I think it's essential that you think through your support systems. By putting them in your business plan, you recognize how important these support systems are to the success of your business.

Few agents entering the business realize that real estate is first a *sales* business. The hardest thing for a salesperson to do is to *stay positive.* Include in your business plan methods to maintain your *sales energy.* Figure 9.8 provides some ideas on support systems. As part of your plan, decide at regular intervals when you will provide yourself motivation, encouragement, recognition and reward—and schedule it. Be ready for those times when you haven't scheduled a "life." Have the resources to find that life when you need it.

Sometimes during my presentations, I ask the students to measure their ability to pat themselves on the back. Many people are uncomfortable with this—they think it's bragging. You don't have to tell anyone else you think you're wonderful—just tell *yourself.* Your success in real estate depends on whether you view yourself as *worthy* of being successful. When you question your worthiness, your self-esteem goes down and with it your self-confidence. Without self-confidence, you can't call effectively on prospects. Without prospects, you can't start the sales cycle. Then, in a vicious circle, your self-esteem gets even lower. So keep your self-esteem high. How? Plan it. Surveys show that people say *ten times more negative things* to themselves (talk to themselves in their heads) than positive things. Test yourself. Today, how many times did you negatively talk to yourself? How many times positively?

Figure 9.7

Support from My Office, Manager and Company

Materials/Resources:_____

_____

_____

_____

Operations: _____

_____

_____

_____

Management Consultation: _____

_____

_____

_____

Training: _____

_____

_____

_____

Other: _____

_____

_____

_____

_____

_____

Figure 9.8

Supporting *You*

Motivational tapes

Motivational books

Motivational courses (Pacific Institute, Seattle, is excellent)

Inspirational sayings/poetry/articles

Listing your accomplishments and reading your list every day

Daily diary

Support partner/family

Shopping (it works for me!)

Self-collected book of sayings/articles that get you "up"

Developing ability to ask for a compliment/accept a compliment

Laughing at the absurdity of a situation instead of at the seriousness of it

Taking time to enjoy the rest of your life (taking art courses, music lessons, etc.)

 You've heard the saying, "We become what we think about." Train yourself to think positive thoughts and to say positive things to yourself. Then, you will find others saying positive things about you!

Summary

Although marketing is the largest part of your business plan, there are other areas that you need to plan for:

- Support systems, including assistants and processes
- Professional development, including courses and organizations
- Self-support—motivating, recognizing and rewarding

Develop yourself in these areas to accomplish your overall sales strategy. By planning for each area, you will not only attain our monetary goals but the personal and professional growth that signifies quality service, high customer satisfaction level and industry enhancement.

10

A Word to Managers

"As an owner, I'm anxious to get **The Real Estate Agent's Business Planning Guide** *into the hands of my agents. It will not only increase agents' productivity, but job satisfaction and client service as well."*

—**Julie Davis**

In This Chapter •

What the system will do for you

Introducing the plan in your office

Meeting with each agent

Mistakes to avoid

Using the plan to build your office

It's relatively easy to understand an idea. It's another matter to explain and teach it to others! I learned this from personal experience. I took all the courses leading to the CRB designation for managers. I thought I understood all the concepts presented. Then I became a CRB instructor—and really learned the difference between understanding and using (or teaching)! And that is why I empathize with managers as they attempt to translate their enthusiasm about an idea to their agents. Introducing a new concept to the agents in our office can be intimidating. With this in mind, I will provide you enough information and confidence in this system to help you successfully use it. In this chapter, I will provide a step-by-step plan to introduce the system to your agents—both in a group setting and/or individually. I have used this system both ways and in various combinations of office and personal planning.

Why Bother with Business Planning?

Your agents *want* business planning. It's the ticket to business success in the '90s. Right now, your agents are searching for a way to *plan their businesses.* They go to seminars. They buy tapes and materials. According to a survey that I conducted of very successful agents, the most important aspect of their career development was *business planning.* And they wanted more in-depth help from their managers in planning and reviewing plans. Following are some responses:

"I think I did not get on track with real estate until I followed my goals and business plan. Even though we learned to write plans in training school, I needed help in implementing and measuring the results of the plan. It wasn't until I believed in myself and my plan that business started to flow."—from a very successful agent, at the end of her first year

"My advice to all agents: Write a business plan every year, allow for flexibility, and live by it."—from an agent in my office who used this system and attained recognition in the top ten percent of a 600-agent company her third year

You: Business Consultant

Agents explore many resources to get help on planning. But, without your help, they will miss the most important ingredient to a successful business: *A knowledgeable consultant.* Without a consultant, writing a business plan is simply a lonely exercise in filling in the blanks. You, the manager, can be that consultant—in fact, you *should* be that consultant. You know the market trends, area characteristics, the agent's strengths and needs. Your perspective on that agent's business is *invaluable.* You just have to communicate that perspective to the agent. In this chapter, I will show you how to introduce the concept of a consultant to your agents—and how to get them excited and motivated to participate in the planning process and review with *you.*

What the System Will Do for the Manager

End the futility of goal-setting. You know the exercise: The manager calls the agent into the office, has him fill out a form with numbers, chats with the agent and puts the form in the agent's personnel file. A few months later, if the agent does not attain his goals, the manager has a stern discussion with the agent—get results or else. This goal-setting process is frustrating for the manager because it leaves him or her with little except *results (closings)* to praise, monitor or redirect. In addition, agents find the goal-setting exercise futile:

1. Goal-setting focuses on numbers of end results. These results are so few and far down the road that agents forget what they wanted to accomplish! (The latest NAR figures show that REALTORS® average only 13 transactions per year per agent. That's only 1 result per month.) An agent's challenge isn't defining what he or she wants as a result—it's planning exactly how to get there.

2. Goal-setting is numbers-based. But an agent's everyday business is *activity-based.* Agents make decisions every day about *what to do.* Without a planning method that helps agents to define the "whats," agents do not know how to plan their days because they have not related daily activities to results.

In contrast, this business planning system provides both the manager and the agent with the process that relates to an agent's *daily activities.* Through this system, the agent can translate the activity portion of his plan into his daily planner. It gives the agent a *purpose* to the activities he intends to complete in his or her day.

Using a Business Planning System

Too many times, agents expect managers to be there when they need them—to be the "walking dictionary" of problem solving. In truth, managers can be much more than that to the agent. Managers can help agents create and implement a powerful business plan. Managers can meet with agents on a consultative basis to measure the results of the plan, suggest adjustments and celebrate the outcomes of the plan. For managers to become consultants, they must substitute a different "trigger" for their meetings with agents—different than a crisis. A more positive trigger, and one that you can orchestrate, is "business planning"—a forward look at the business, rather than the piecemeal, fix-it approach that comes from crisis management.

How To Introduce the Plan

As an agent, did you like to go through the exercise of goal-setting? I didn't. In fact, I remember that I gave my manager whatever I thought he wanted to hear. I didn't understand that the objective was to *plan*—and that

Figure 10.1

Have a Say in Our Office Direction Next Year!

Join us, as we put our heads together to analyze the challenges and opportunities of our market. Working together, we can begin the process to:

Put Together the Office Plan
Put Together Our Individual Plans

In today's complex, quickly changing market, we need more minds than one to recognize the possibilities that crop up each day. We'll look at:
* National market trends that may affect our area
* Political, economic, environmental challenges that may affect our business
* Demographic and psychographic profiles of our target markets, and how changes in these variables affect our business
* Business competitors, and the opportunities for our growth
* Company and office trends and developments that will affect our businesses

Bring Any Information or Helpful Statistics to Our Workshop!!!!

We'll draw conclusions on the challenges and opportunities afforded in these areas, while relating them to our office and our personal businesses.

Our meetings are: _____

Suggestions? See me! Thanks for your participation!

---

it was to my benefit! Most agents feel the same way. They don't want to take the time to plan. Knowing that, you need to carefully introduce this idea, get the agents interested in the concept and motivate them to create their plans. In implementing this planning system in my office, I use a four-step process:

Step 1:   Announce in a meeting that you will be introducing this planning idea during a special session, to be held for two hours outside your normal meeting day. Start this process in early November in order to help your agents do an analysis of the area and market trends in preparation for starting their own planning process.

In your meeting announcement, be sure to address concerns of a changing market, the need for a personal plan and how you will help each agent design a plan customized for his or her use.

Step 2:   Present a workshop of the analysis of market trends. Gather information and analyze the past in order to predict the future. The agent, as well as the entire office staff, needs to address the opportunities and challenges of your particular market area. I use a general workshop to explore these opportunities and challenges. Later, when I create the office plan, I use this same information. (The office plan and each agent's plan should be *complementary*.) In the workshop, I relate this information to each of the agent's plans.

To introduce the workshop and get agents interested, prepare a flyer. Figure 10.2 is an agenda for the planning workshop, including guides for facilitating the workshop.

Step 3: Explain how the agent's personal business planning system works. This explanation can be done by having the agent read this book. Or you can give a short workshop on the planning process.

Step 4: Meet with each agent to go over his or her plan. Set aside one to two hours for each agent. This is a critical step because you are starting your new relationship with your agents as a *business consultant*. This first consulting session forms the basis, too, for your continued business meetings in the future. In your counseling session, you will go through the following process:

- Ask the agent to analyze his or her past business, using the business analysis sheets provided. Ask the agent what changes he or she wants to make in his business next year, based on this analysis. Note the replies.

- Check the agent's objectives and his or her "pacing" of these objectives throughout the year. Be sure that the agent does not plan to sell more homes in December than in March.

- Check the target markets to be sure that the agent is really going to work the best sources of business (past customers and clients). Check to see that there are reasonable numbers of results and contacts, that there are enough target markets or numbers in those markets to get results and that these markets fit into the office plan.

- Check the tactics for each target market to be sure that there is a time frame, a mini-plan for each tactic (or one to be developed) and a budget attached for each tactic.

End of Session Summary: At the end of your meeting with each agent, add any redirection needed, and close with plenty of positive reinforcement. Get a copy of the business plan, and explain to the agent that you will regularly review these plans—focusing on the *tactics* (everyday activities), *not just the results.* You will use these plans to frame ongoing consulting sessions and to put together teams or pairs of agents who want to increase their businesses from particular markets. You will also review the plans to see how you can help the agent with special needs, resources or sales techniques. This is how *you'll be accountable to the agents in your office.*

Figure 10.2

Agenda: Planning Workshop (2–3 hours)

Introduction: Why a planning workshop?
What we'll do today—and how we'll do it
How to use this information for your own planning process
(Note to manager: Bring area market statistics, plus any market trend information you have available, to this workshop. Prepare each task force by giving them copies of this information.)

Analyzing Market Trends

Task Force Exercise: Directions—divide the attendees into "task forces" of no more than six people. Name a reporter for each group. Assign each task force an area, as listed below (list these on an overhead transparency or flip chart). The task force discusses trends in this area and draws conclusions of challenges and opportunities these trends indicate. Task force reporter prepares a 3-minute report to the whole group, as well as a written report. Task forces have 20–30 minutes to work. *Give these directions to the attendees twice before you ask them to get into groups!*

Task Force Topics:
*   International and national political, economic, environmental trends
*   Regional and local political, economic, environmental trends
*   Target markets: trends, demographic and psychographic variables
*   Company and office trends
*   Competitors—trends

Each task force discusses *one* topic only, drawing conclusions about the challenges and opportunities it sees in the trends and emerging developments.

After attendees have worked in task forces for 20–30 minutes, tell them to stay in their groups but prepare the report—verbally and in writing.

Reports: Have each reporter report to the whole group. Then ask all attendees for any more comments on this topic (hold discussion to five minutes). Gather the written reports, and have your secretary type all these reports for your agents' use in their own planning processes.

Conclusions: With the whole group, discuss applications to the office and to the agent's individual plan.

How To Use the Plan in Ongoing Sessions

One of the most difficult things for managers to do is ongoing consulting. In fact, most managers just don't do it. And, when managers have to rely on the information provided by goal-setting (generally just numbers), it's not much fun to meet with agents! The business planning system provides so much in-depth information that you will have abundant information for four to eight consulting sessions per year. Here are some ideas about how to organize these sessions:

- Simply have meetings with each agent on the progress of his business plan. Focus on the tactics and their relationship to the target markets and results. Provide positive reinforcement for activities and helpful consulting. Ask permission to share some of the successful tactics with others in a workshop or general sales meeting.

- Use a theme of past customers and clients to organize a session. Then gather the tactics of the agents and conduct a workshop, sharing ideas in this gold mine for customers and clients.

- Use a theme of certain performances that add to results. Be sure to announce to all agents the particular theme for the consulting session far enough in advance for the agents to practice, prepare and improve. For example, one of the most common evaluations agents make about themselves in the business analysis is that they could be better at qualifying buyers. Using this theme, ask each agent how he improved his qualifying method since the first of the year.

- Using the form in Figure 11.6, ask each agent to project his or her expected earnings for the next three-month period. I started using this approach when I began managing my office—rates were 20 percent. I needed to know the potential of each agent in order to make some personnel decisions. You will find this method useful in separating borderline agents and deciding who should go "up" or "out."

A Manager's Checklist

To be successful, all plans should include the following:

- Analysis and recognition of market trends that indicate the agent should change his or her business strategies.

- Analysis of the agent's particular business strategies, with recommendations for changes in business strategies.

- Agent's focus or vision to position himself or herself to relate to his or her particular business plan.

- Measurable objectives expressed in units.

- Targets: Particular target markets, always starting with the best markets—the agent's past customers and clients—with enough potentials in each market to bring the desired results. Targets must be prioritized according to ability to deliver adequate sales and listings sold to meet objectives. They must be the best markets for the agent.

- Tactics, which should be:
  - related specifically to particular target markets.
  - frequent enough to get business from market.
  - consistent enough to be cohesive with other tactics and consistent to the needs and characteristics of that market.
  - accompanied by a budget figure; the whole budget is added up for each market and added up for all markets.
  - have people assigned to complete each task.
  - have dates for completion of each task.

All plans must include the following:

- Systems for measuring the effectiveness of the tactics.
- Consistency overall.
- Frequency to each target market.
- Promotional and action-oriented nature.
- Personal promotional tactics related to specific target markets.

A good business plan is a reflection of that particular agent's strengths and talents, apparent in meaningful action steps.

Summary

At a recent NAR Convention, I organized a panel of *supermanagers*. During this panel discussion, I asked the 350 attendees which was their major concern: recruiting or productivity.

The majority replied: *productivity*. And the best way to build productivity is to focus your agents' efforts on developing their individual businesses. There are several benefits to this *refocus*:

- Agents get excited about their own ability to find leads.
- Agents get creative about tactics that they can employ.
- Agents allocate their own marketing dollars well because they know they have strategies to get results from the money spent.
- Agents look to the manager as a valuable leader, valued for his consulting services.
- Agents become mentors to other agents because they have confidence in their abilities to analyze and redirect associates.

The bottom line is: *Managers have more fun managing!*

CHAPTER

11

Managing Your Plan for Success

"These planning worksheets have been very valuable to me. The system is a must for any serious agent."

—Tom Reed

In This Chapter •

Organizing your plan

Reviewing tour plan

Projecting future business

Your next plan

A Practical *Daily* Plan of Attack

This book provides a lot of information. How do you organize it so that you actually get to your work each day, doing the things that make a difference in your career? The easiest way is to use a monthly calendar (see Figure 11.1). Note on your calendar the following goals and activities:

- Your objectives (sales, listings sold, listings and referrals out)
- Your desired level of sales activities (prospecting, listing appointments, showings)
- Your marketing tactics (tactical marketing moves from your marketing circles)
- Your tactics from your professional development section

Figure 11.1

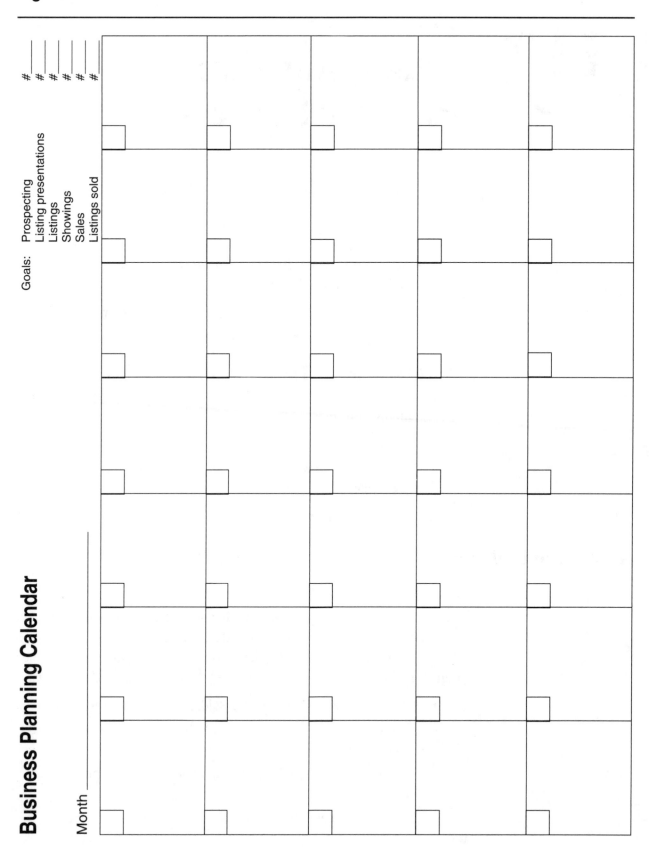

Your Objectives

First, put your objectives—the results that you want to accomplish—at the top of your calendar. You noted these objectives on the worksheet in Figure 5.8. Since you already plotted *when* you wanted to accomplish each of these objectives, you only need to transfer this information to your calendar.

Desired Level of Sales Activities

Mini-objectives are the activities that you must do in large numbers—consistently—to be sure that you get the results you want. Use the numbers you filled in Figure 5.13. Figure 11.2 is similar, but it has added grids for goals and actuals so that you can measure your successes. This will give you the numbers of sales-producing activities that you need to accomplish during that month to guarantee the results you want.

Your Marketing Tactics

As I mentioned previously, most business planning systems for agents only plot the *numbers* needed for success. In actuality, it's the particular targeted *specific activities* that you accomplish in your marketing plan that ensure your effectiveness. Thus, you should add to your calendar all the tactical moves that you planned on your targeted marketing circles. Use either the circles that you completed or the tactical itemization sheet to get your calendar dates (see Chapter 7).

Your Moves in Your Professional Development

Now add the priorities you decided on from your professional development section (see Chapter 9). Be sure to prioritize the most important activities you want to accomplish—*in relationship to their importance to your overall planning strategy.*

A typical monthly calendar is illustrated in Figure 11.3.

The Ultimate Measurement System

The greatest challenge in writing this book was deciding how much detail to include. In reality, most real estate salespeople are not *detail* people. However, as you can see, when you run your own business, you must pay attention to details—as well as the big picture. To help you, I've provided planning grids for specific needs (e.g., tactical planning worksheet)

Figure 11.2

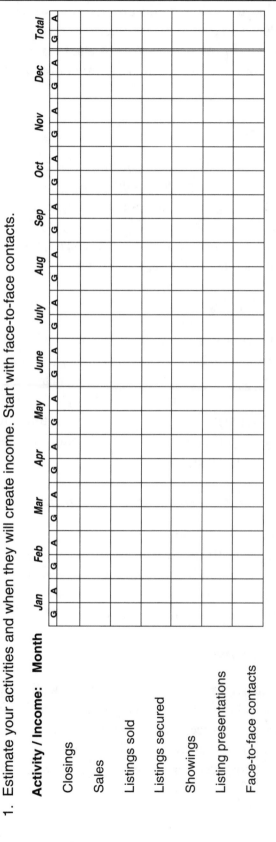

Activities, Expenses, Results, Profits

1. Estimate your activities and when they will create income. Start with face-to-face contacts.

Activity / Income: Month	Jan		Feb		Mar		Apr		May		June		July		Aug		Sep		Oct		Nov		Dec		Total	
	G	A	G	A	G	A	G	A	G	A	G	A	G	A	G	A	G	A	G	A	G	A	G	A	G	A
Closings																										
Sales																										
Listings sold																										
Listings secured																										
Showings																										
Listing presentations																										
Face-to-face contacts																										

2. Tally your expenses per month. Log in your projected earnings and "paids."

Business expenses												
Earned income (written)												
Paid income (closed)												
Profit per month												
Profit (year-to-date)												

G = Goal
A = Actual

Figure 11.3

Business Planning Calendar

Month _____ January _____

Goals:
Prospecting	# 200
Listing presentations	# 4
Listings	# 2
Showings	# 6
Sales	# 1
Listings sold	# 1

1	**2** Prepare card for past clients	**3** Call 5 past customers	**4** Sign up for prep. broker class	**5** Mail card to 100 past clients	**6** Circle prospect 50 homes
7 Hold open house	**8** Broker prep. class	**9**	**10** Call 5 past customers	**11** Broker prep. class	**12** Call 5 FSBOs	**13** Circle prospect 50 homes
14 Hold open house	**15** Broker prep. class	**16**	**17** Call 5 past customers	**18** Broker prep. class	**19** Follow up 5 FSBOs	**20** Circle prospect 50 homes
21 Hold open house	**22** Broker prep. class	**23**	**24** Call 5 past customers	**25** Prepare PR statement & mail	**26** Follow-up 5 FSBOs	**27** Circle prospect 50 homes
28 Hold open house	**29** Call 5 past customers	**30** Create home office	**31** Broker prep. class		

and measurement systems for specific marketing moves (e.g., promotion comparison worksheet). However, the most important planning grid in this book is the one entitled "Activities, Results, Expenses and Profits" (Figure 11.2). With all the concepts in this book on one sheet of paper, you can easily set goals for your business and keep track of results. You can see how your expenses accrue through time and how your activities lead to *earned* income and, later on, *paid* income. You can see how your budget is impacted through time by your results and how profitable you are month to month, and year to date.

The Race: Your Time and Money Against Results

The most common problem for new agents is that their money runs out before they get a sales result. In addition, they lose heart in the business because they do not get results fast enough. Every time I tracked the business activities of a new agent that failed, I found that the new agent actually refused to *start the business.* That is, the new agent did not make enough sales calls to produce an adequate number of listing and showing appointments to get a sale—before his energy and money ran out. The new agent was busy—doing what I call *support activities.* However, doing support activities without talking to people is an exercise in futility. The beauty of this timeline is that it shows agents how activities relate to results *through time.*

Help for the "Slumping" Agent

I teach many business planning courses. It always amazes me when slumping agents (those whose productivity has gone down alarmingly)—really do not know what the problem is. That is, they do not have the analytical tools to figure out why they are in a slump. If agents had set goals in the areas we have just discussed and measured their results, they would know the adjustments that must be made to ensure the results they want. In addition, many slumping agents have created a job description of themselves *as their own assistant*—doing all the support activities that should be delegated to someone else. This is a convenient way of avoiding doing sales activities—and it also ensures low results. By simply following the principles in this business planning guide, any agent can pull himself or herself out of a slumping career. For more detailed information on analyzing activities, see *Up and Running in 30 Days.*

One-Page Business Management

To easily manage your business plan, set goals and keep track of your actual statistics using Figure 11.2. First, set your goals.

At the top of the timeline:

- Put your prospecting activities through time on the timeline.
- Decide on the mini-objectives you want (listing presentations, showings). Put these through time on the timeline.
- Put your objectives (from Figure 5 .8) on the timeline.

At the bottom of the timeline:

- Put your business expenses per month (from Figure 5.4).
- Project your earned income (using average commission). This is directly below where you listed *sales* or *listings sold. Earned* means that you wrote an offer that was signed both ways or that your listing just had an offer signed both ways.
- Project your *closed* income. This means the home has closed and you received a check. Be sure your timeframes are reasonable.
- Subtract your expenses from your closed income to get your monthly profitability.
- Add your profitability per month to get your profitability-to-date.

You have your goals for the year—on one piece of paper. Monthly, log in your actual activities, results, expenses and profit. You can see if you are reaching your career objectives—on one piece of paper.

Reviewing Your Plan at Regular Intervals

You have set your goals and are keeping track of your results monthly. Actually, you are reviewing your progress monthly. In addition, you need to review all facets of your plan, including your marketing moves, at least quarterly. Here are the specific areas to review:

- Management by the numbers
    - Activities and results to date from Figure 11.2
    - Expenses vs. income vs. profitability

Figure 11.4

Business Plan Three-Month Review

Quarterly goals: Listings Taken _____   For months _____

Listings Sold _____

Sales _____

1. **Management by the Numbers**

    My analysis of my activities/results to date: _____

    _____

    My analysis of my expenses/profitability to date: _____

    _____

    Adjustments I need to make: _____

    _____

2. **Marketing**

    My analysis of my results from specific target markets: _____

    _____

    My analysis of my specific promotional tactics effectiveness: _____

    _____

    Changes I need to make: _____

    _____

3. **Professional Development**

    My analysis of my accomplishments: _____

    _____

    Adjustments I need to make: _____

    _____

4. **The Big Picture**

    Does my stated focus match the results of my activities and my overall business

    objectives for this year? _____ Adjustments I need to make:_____

    _____

    _____

- Marketing
  - Results from specific target markets
  - Specific promotional tactics effectiveness (refer to Figure 7.11)
  - Professional development
  - The big picture
  - Your stated focus vs. the results of your activities
  - Your overall business objectives for that year

Use worksheet Figure 11.4 to review your plans quarterly and make adjustments.

Projecting and Predicting Future Business

When I started managing my first office, interest rates were 20 percent. The market had changed radically, but most of the agents had not adjusted their businesses to take advantage of the market change. As I talked with agents, I sensed that they were waiting for something to happen, rather than making something happen. To find out what their future businesses might look like, I created the worksheet shown in Figure 11.5. This is a valuable tool for projecting your business. Use it to make adjustments in your business plan *before* you find yourself with inadequate listing appointments, listings or selling appointments. Use it to predict your immediate sources of income.

Let's take a look first at *listings now*. Log in your listings and probable sale and close date, congruent with the state of your market. Put this potential income at the bottom of the sheet, which is a timeline. Do the same for listings in the future. Be sure to project enough time to ensure that these listings enjoy average market time in your area. Last, log in people you are working with now. Evaluate them for probable purchase date and the date their home will close. Now you have a good idea of your future sources of income. Are these sources sufficient to reach your objectives? If not, go back and start the sales cycle (see Figure 9.2). Create a dynamic prospecting plan to find prospects and qualify them. Review the marketing portion of your business plan. Be sure that you are meeting and re-meeting enough people in each target market to guarantee adequate business flow to you.

Figure 11.5

Review of Business and Projections

Use this worksheet to project your earnings for a specific time period. _____

Name: _____ Date: _____ Review period, from: _____ to _____

Paid to date: _____ Earned to date: _____

Listings now:

Seller's Name	Home Price	Priced Right?	Probable Sell Date	Probable Close Date	Your Commission

Listings in the future that you know you'll list during this analysis period:

Seller's Name	Home Price	Priced Right?	Probable Sell Date	Probable Close Date	Your Commission

People you're working with now:

Buyer's Name	Buyer's Price Range	Priced Right?	Probable Buy Date	Probable Close Date	Your Commission

Total commissions you expect to be paid (business that you know you'll have) for the rest of this year: _____

Put your commissions earned and paid on this timeline. Start with the present month and work to the end of the time period requested. Then you can see your potential income over time and revise your business plan/budget as needed.

Month: _____ _____ _____ _____ _____ _____

Will Earn: _____ _____ _____ _____ _____ _____

Will Be Paid: _____ _____ _____ _____ _____ _____

Getting Help with Your Business Reviews

All agents have the best of intentions as they create our business plan. However, life frequently gets in the way, and they forget to review their plans. Sometimes they forget to follow their plans. However, the fact is that those who follow *any* thought-out plan do better than those who don't. To be sure that you take the time to review your plan: First, find an agent that is about in the same stage of his/her career as you are. Arrange to be each other's consultants as you make and review the plan. Then, you will not only have a reason to review your plan, but you will provide important consulting help to your associate.

Ask Your Manager To Help You Review

By now, you realize that your manager can be of great help in making and reviewing your business plan. Managers can provide great insights—if asked. But think how much more powerful the plan can be if it captures the synergy of the office and company and is supported by management. Enlist your manager's help in reviewing your plan.

Your Planning Checklist

Figure 11.6 provides a checklist to ensure that you have written a plan that will work. The checklist is in the order in which you designed your plan. Using the checklist, go back over the parts of your plan to be sure that you have taken advantage of the interlocking nature of a good plan. That is:

- marketing tactics support each other;
- marketing tactics support your personal style;
- performance standards are imbued in each part of your plan; and
- you, your office and your company plans are synergistic.

Planning Mistakes

Some people are better at knowing what not to do than at knowing what *to do.* Use the checklist in Figure 11.7 as a reference for double-checking your plan. Armed with these two checklists and the systems inherent in this planning method, you can create a dynamic business plan to reach your objectives.

Figure 11.6

Planning Checklist To Ensure a System for Success

☐ Market trends are recognized and integrated into the plan.

☐ Your business analysis indicates changes you want to make. Those changes are integrated into your plan.

☐ Your vision gives you your "position" in the marketplace. Your position is reflected in your choice of target markets; your tactics reflect your focus.

☐ Your vision is in sync with that of your office and company.

☐ Your objectives are true end results: listings sold and sales, along with other measurable objectives to expand your business.

☐ You are focused on units, not $.

☐ You want to increase your business, not just your income.

☐ You start with your best target market and have fully planned number of tactics for that market.

☐ You have enough "potentials" in your target market to ensure results.

☐ You have a clear idea of how many sales/listings sold you'll get from each market.

☐ Your tactics are related to a particular target market.

☐ You know why you're doing each tactic.

☐ Your tactics are consistent and frequent to a particular market.

☐ Your personalized marketing efforts are expressed as tactics, related to particular markets.

☐ Each of your tactics has a budget, work assignments and date for completion.

☐ You concentrate on making a profit, not just on being productive.

☐ You have set up methods to measure the results of your promotional tactics.

☐ You have put your tactics on a calendar so you can assign yourself daily activities.

☐ You have a method to measure your successes along the way.

Figure 11.7

Checklist: Agent Planning Mistakes

☐ No cohesive campaign to impact each target market. (Theme needs to pervade campaign.)

☐ One promotional piece sent once to thousands of strangers.

☐ No target market defined.

☐ No budget attached to specific markets.

☐ Wrong target markets chosen (best–past customers).

☐ No dates for completion of tactics.

☐ Too few impacts on target markets (six minimum needed per year).

☐ No overall budget.

☐ Competition not defined or respected (plan not strong enough to take market share from competition).

☐ Numbers only—no defined plan for reaching these numbers.

☐ Plan not consistent with particular individual's business (all pizza parlors don't use the same plan).

☐ Little analysis done of outside conditions.

☐ Little internal analysis done—no analysis of needs to refine plan.

☐ Individual doesn't thoroughly define his "position" in the marketplace prior to creating promotions.

☐ Promotional plan not related to particular market.

☐ Activities not delegated properly.

Summary

Congratulations! You have completed your business plan. You are on your way to a profitable year as a pro. You have learned to look at your business from some different perspectives, which gives you a distinct advantage.

After you have used this planning system the first time, you will find the process goes much faster in succeeding years. All you need to do to begin the process again is to give yourself an update on the external and internal business analysis. You don't need to redo your vision. Simply proceed from your business review to the objectives, marketing and professional development parts of your plan.

Not only will you reap the benefits of planning, your customers and clients will, too. Your planning enterprise is directly applicable to their selling and buying processes. Use this concept to promote yourself and your services. You've earned it!

Sample Business Plans

. . . .

In this section, I have provided two sample business plans:

1. For the agent in his or her first year of business, establishing his or her business

2. For the agent in his or her second to fourth year in the business, growing his or her business to the desired level

I chose these plans because most agents fall into these two categories.

Using this business planning system can save the first-year agent many frustrations: Missed business opportunities because of lack of focus, too few or too many marketing dollars spent, and the feelings that come from being "adrift" on the sea of real estate activities.

For the high-growth agent, this business plan provides many benefits: Using this thought process, the growth agent can refine his plan, dedicate his marketing dollars to activities that assure the "biggest bang for the buck," and reap the benefits that accrue from designing a plan based on his or her proven real estate strengths.

What about the "superstar" agent? Although we hear much about the marketing tactics of the superstar agent, in reality, less than one percent of the total agents selling real estate reach superstar status (closing over $10 million in volume in one year).

Another reason I haven't included a business plan of the superstar agent is that, in reality, most agents today do not want to reach superstar status.

They want to hear superstar strategies, but they don't want to expend the effort or money to attain the results. So, let's be realistic. Let's provide real plans for real people.

What's in this book for the superstar? The principles in this book will help you to more effectively refine, focus and spend your marketing dollars. This system will help you to take the ideas you pick up from other superstars and translate them to your overall "big picture business plan." Instead of being confused about which great tactical idea to pursue, you can determine the best ideas for you. You can translate Joe's techniques that were successful on the east coast to plans that will work for Susan on the west coast.

Here's the organization of these sample plans. First, I will describe each agent to help you understand his or his particular career moves and planning tactics. I will use the most important forms provided in your planner to create a business plan for each agent.

Samantha Smith

Personal History. Samantha, a former elementary teacher, lives in a residential area near a golf course. She used to teach in the school that serves this area. Samantha is married to an attorney; they have two grade-school-age children.

Personality Profile. From Samantha's teaching career, she exhibited the qualities of nurturing and support. She doesn't like to be pushed into decisions and looks at herself as a counselor.

Personal Strengths. Writing ability, teaching ability and creative methods to motivate people are among Samantha's strengths. She has a very supportive attitude toward people.

Memberships and Activities. She is a member of the golf club and is active in her church.

Real Estate History. In the real estate business six months, Samantha has enjoyed a good, fast start. (See her internal situation analysis for the specifics.) She feels she has learned the basics and wants to create an overall plan to take her to the next level—a solid, growing business. Samantha completed a total of six sales and listings sold her first six months in the business (the national average for sales and listings sold for all

REALTORS® in all experience levels is 6.75 in a six-month period). Samantha enjoyed higher productivity during these first six months than most first-year agents. She wants to maintain and increase her momentum. Samantha's market is a very competitive, large area where transferees make up 25 percent of the total business.

Samantha created her plan in her seventh month in the business. Although she has done enough business to use her personal sales statistics, her second and third years' plans will *really* provide her the history and guidance she needs to build a dynamic career.

A Review of Your Business

Sales __3__   Listings taken (LT) __6__

Listings sold (LS) __3__   % of LT to LS __50%__

Average time on market for your listings __45 days__ (Break down by price range if desired)

% of sales price to list price for your listings __97%__   Number of new listings sold __0__

Number of resales sold __3__   Number of resale listings sold __3__

Number of new homes sold __0__

Origination of Buyers/Sellers		
	Buyers	Sellers
Reactive Prospecting		
Floor time	1	1
Open houses		1
Proactive Prospecting (Segmented by Target Market)		
Past customers/clients		
First-time buyers		
Move-up buyers		
Transferees		
Empty-nesters		
Geographical farm		
Prior business contacts		1
Builders		
Other _people I know_	2	3

Of these sellers, which market gave you the most sold listings?

☞   **Keep exploiting these markets. They're your most effective.**

Analysis: Your Business Strengths and Challenges

Rate yourself as: 1 = Excellent 2 = Very Good

3 = Fair 4 = Needs Improvment

Activity	Rating
Sales	
Finding potential buyers (proactive)	3
Evaluating buying potential	2
Following up with potential buyers	2
Interviewing, qualifying buyers, building rapport	2
Showing properties buyers want to see	2
Helping buyers make buying decisions—closing	3
Evaluating time spent in helping each buyer (too much, not enough?)	4

Activity	Rating
Listing	
Finding potential sellers (proactive)	3
Qualifying sellers	3
Evaluating marketability of product	3
Giving an effective listing presentation	2
Closing for a listing	2
Promoting property	2
Time on market for my properties	3

Activity	Rating
Skills/Operations	
Counseling skills with buyers	2
Negotiating the earnest money agreement	2
Follow-up prior to closing	1
Follow-up after closing—building referral business	2
Distribution plan for marketing myself	3
Telephone skills	3
Open house skills	3

Main goals: *Better proactive prospecting*
Better ongoing marketing programs
Better sales skills

Samantha Smith

Vision Statement. I am a residential specialist serving the greater eastside area. I specialize in helping families move in and out of the area, or to move up within the eastside area. My strengths include the ability to communicate effectively, to market properties with my writing skills, and to give buyers and sellers the pertinent information to make the best decisions for them. My credo is to "listen to the concerns of my clients and customers to ensure that their needs are served to their best interests, not mine." In doing so, I create business relationships for life.

Personal Operating Expenses

Regular Monthly Payments

House payments (principal, interest, taxes, insurance, condominium fees or rent) • • •	$	1,000
Car payments (including insurance) •	$	400
Appliance, TV payments •	$	
Home improvement loan payments •	$	
Personal loan, credit card payments •	$	200
Health plan payments •	$	200
Life insurance payments •	$	50
Other insurance payments •	$	
Total •	$	1,850*

Household Operating Expenses

Telephone •	$	50
Gas and electricity •	$	250
Water •	$	50
Other household expenses, repairs, maintenance • • • • • • • • • • • • • • • • • • •	$	200
Total •	$	550

Personal Expenses

Clothing, cleaning, laundry •	$	200
Prescription medications •	$	50
Physicians, dentists •	$	100
Education •	$	50
Dues •	$	25
Gifts and contributions •	$	50
Newspapers, magazines, books •	$	25
Auto upkeep and gas (part may go in your real estate budget) • • • • • • • • • • • • •	$	50
Children's school tuition •	$	
Spending money and allowances •	$	200
Miscellaneous •	$	100
Total •	$	850

Food Expenses

Food—at home •	$	600
Food—away from home •	$	200
Total •	$	800

Tax Expenses

Federal and state income taxes •	$	1,250
Other taxes not included above •	$	100
Total •	$	1,350

Total Personal Monthly Expenses •	$	5,400*
Total Personal Yearly Expenses •	$	64,800

Samantha must earn enough to cover 1/2 of the family expenses, or $32,400 for the year.

Total Marketing Costs and Analysis of % of Gross Income

Transfer your marketing costs for each target market and listing/selling costs to this sheet.

I.   Target Markets to Generate Business

Past customers/clients	$ 385
Geographical farm	$ 600
Prior profession	$ 550
Circle of influence	$
Expired listings	$
FSBOs	$
Other - attorneys	$ 250
Other	$
Other	$
Total	$ 1,785

II.   Listing Costs (Cost Per Listing x Number of Listings)

Signs/name signs	$ 25
Display boxes	$ 10
Flyers/brochures	$ 25
Print advertising	$ 50
Mailings	$ 50
Seller gifts	$ 50
Other	$
Total per listing	$ 210
x ___12___ listings	
Total	$ 2,520

III.   Other Promotions

Gifts	$ 300
Entertainment	$ 500
Personal marketing	
photos	$ 100
brochures	$ 200
graphics	$ 200
printing	$ 200
other	$
Business cards	$ 100
Sponsorships	$ 100
Community service	$ 100
Total	$ 1,800

Total Marketing Expenses	$ 6,105

Total Marketing Expense as a % of Income ___10___ %
(Marketing expense ÷ gross income)

Professional Development

	Date To Accomplish*	Budget*

Courses, Workshops

_____workshops to develop skill		
__✔__Graduate Realtors'® Institute (GRI)	7/94	200
_____Certified Residential Specialist (CRS)		
_____Certified Real Estate Broker (CRB)		
__✔__Realtors'® presentations, workshops	4/94	100
__✔__legal updates	10/94	100
_____technical courses		
_____hours toward broker's license		
_____hours toward continuing education credit		
_____teach real estate course		
_____other		

Books, Tapes

__✔__business books bought and read	ongoing	100
__✔__audiotapes purchased	ongoing	100
_____videos purchased		
_____study programs purchased		
_____other		

Presentations, Processes, Systems

__✔__develop listing presentation marketing manual	3/94	100
__✔__develop buyers' presentation manual	2/94	50
__✔__develop professional portfolio	1/94	50
_____develop seller qualifying system		
_____develop follow-up systems after the sale		
_____other		

Organizations

_____become more active in Realtor® organization		
__✔__attend local Realtor® convention	10/94	100
__✔__attend National Realtor® Convention	11/94	200
_____join Realtor® committee		
__✔__attend company convention	6/94	100
_____other		
	Total Budget:	$ 1,200

*Add these dates to your business plan calendar. Put the budget items in your operating or marketing budget.

Main needs: Increase my professionalism by becoming more skilled in sales.

Systems/Mechanical/Labor Checklist

Choose from the following areas the systems and support you want to plan for this year.

	*Date To Accomplish**	*Budget**
Mechanical		
✔ buy a computer, printer	*6/95*	*2,000*
buy a typewriter		
✔ purchase software programs	*6/95*	*800*
purchase computer hardware		
take lessons on computers		
get voicemail, pager		
purchase car phone		
purchase fax machine		
purchase multiple listing service at home		
other		
Labor		
hire assistant		
hire mailing service		
✔ other *- part-time help*	*1/95*	*600*
Home Office		
✔ office furniture	*6/95*	*300*
office supplies		
fax		
computer/printer		
other		

Total Budget: *$ 3,700*

*Put these dates in your business plan calendar. Add these budget items to your operating budget.

Main goal: To create flyers/mailers to my target markets and hire a part-time assistant to implement plan.

Your Real Estate Budget
Real Estate Operating Expenses

	Yearly	Monthly
Total marketing budget	$ 6,105	$ 509
Professional fees (REALTORS®, MLS)	$ 1,000	$ 83
Business car expenses (gas, oil, tools, repair)	$ 2,400	$ 200
Communications expenses (pager, phone)	$ 1,200	$ 100
Labor/mechanical (from systems worksheet)	$ 3,700	$ 308
Professional development (from worksheet)	$ 1,200	$ 100
Supplies	$ 1,200	$ 100
Business insurance	$ 200	$ 17
Legal fees	$ 400	$ 33
Licenses, permits	$ 100	$ 8
Other	$	$
Total	$ 17,505	$ 1,459

Deciding the Profit You Want

Total dollars from Personal Operating Expenses _____ $ 32,400

Total dollars from Real Estate Operating Expenses _____ 17,505

Dreams/fun _____ 500

Total $ needed to cover total expenses | 50,405

Desired profit _____ 10,000*

Grand total of dollars you want to earn | $ 60,405

*Samantha knows she must invest in her business to build a long-term career. She wants a profit of $10,000 to show that she has accomplished her goals—and she's setting the stage for a dynamic career.

Overall Objectives

Name: _Samantha Smith_   Office: _Western Realty_

Date Completed: _6/94_   For Year: _July '94 - June '95_

Your average commission per sale/listing sold (S/LS) = $ _2,700††_

Your past year's ratio of sales written to sales closed _85_ %   Your past year's ratio of LT/LS= _50_ %

Your next year's desired ratio _80_ %   Your next year's ratio of listings sold to sales _50_ %

Listings:

Number of listings taken (units) _12_

Number of listings sold (units) _10_ x average commission = $ _2,700_ – sales fails ($_2,700_) = $ _24,300_ net income

Sales:

Number of sales (units) _12_ x average commission = $ _32,400_ – sales fails ($_2,700_) = $ _29,700_ net income

Referrals out:

Number of referrals (units) _12_ x average commission = $ _6,000_ – sales fails ($ ——) = $ _6,000_ net income

Totals:

Total net revenue units + (LS/S) = [_22_]   Total net commissions paid = $ [_60,000_] *

L = Listing   * paid in that year
LS = Listing Sold   + a revenue unit = a listing sold or a sale
S = Sale

††Assumes Samantha has a graduated split program

Setting Objectives for Sales Effectiveness

Of all the areas that you analyzed and want to change and/or improve, which are the most important to you to increase your business effectiveness?

☑ Change ratio of listings taken to listings sold from _50_ % to _80_ %.

☐ Change ratio of listings sold to sales from _____ % to _____ %.

☑ Change listing time on market from _45_ average days to _30_ average days.

☐ Increase average commission by changing price range for listings from $ _____ to $ _____ .

☐ Change price range for sales to increase average commission from $ _____ to $ _____ .

☑ To reduce number of showings per sale to _5_ .

☑ Change ratio of listing presentations to listings that sell from _40_ % to _70_ %.

☑ Switch from _50_ % proactive methods to find buyers/sellers to _75_ %.

These priorities for your overall sales strategy will provide the basis for your marketing and professional development plans.

Choose Your Target Markets

1. Fill in the top portion of each circle with a name of a potential target (past customers and clients, geographical farm, FSBO, expired listings, certain professions, etc.).

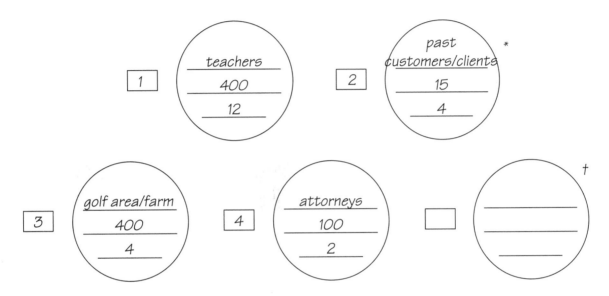

2. Estimate the number of potential contacts in each market by filling the middle blank in each circle (prospecting).

3. Estimate the number of listings sold and sales derived from this market by filling in the bottom portion of the circle.

4. Prioritize the importance of these markets to you by numbering the market in the box (#1 is your best market).

Example:

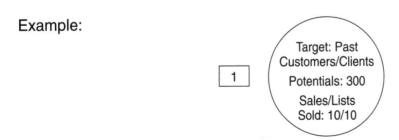

* Will become #1 as Samantha's career matures (by her third full year)

† Samantha thinks she has enough potentials in these markets to deliver her objectives. She'll also be taking floor time and open houses to supplement her proactive plan.

Create Business-Producing Tactics for Your Target Market

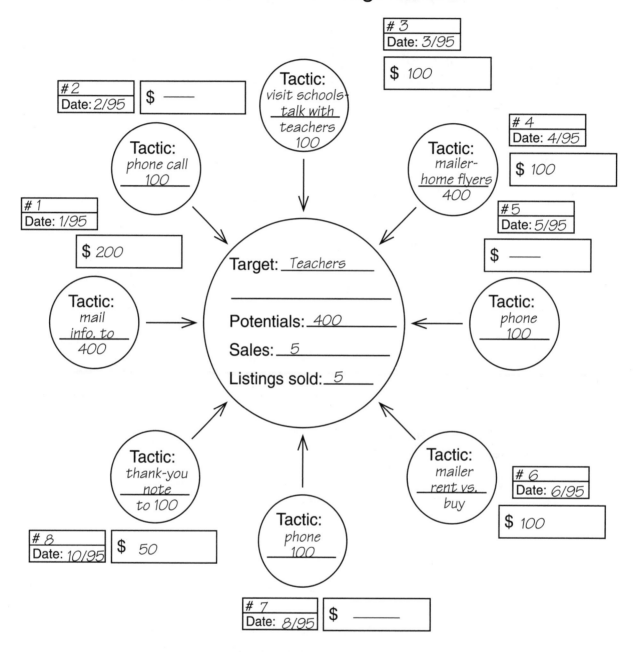

Total tactical impact (number of in-person/telephone): _400_ (transfer to Figure 6.6.)

Total budget for this market: $ _550_ . Add this budget to your total marketing budget.

Main messages: *I understand your needs - I am a teacher.*
I am a successful agent - you can count on me.
I provide the best information to you. *Ask for referrals.*

Create Business-Producing
Tactics for Your Target Market

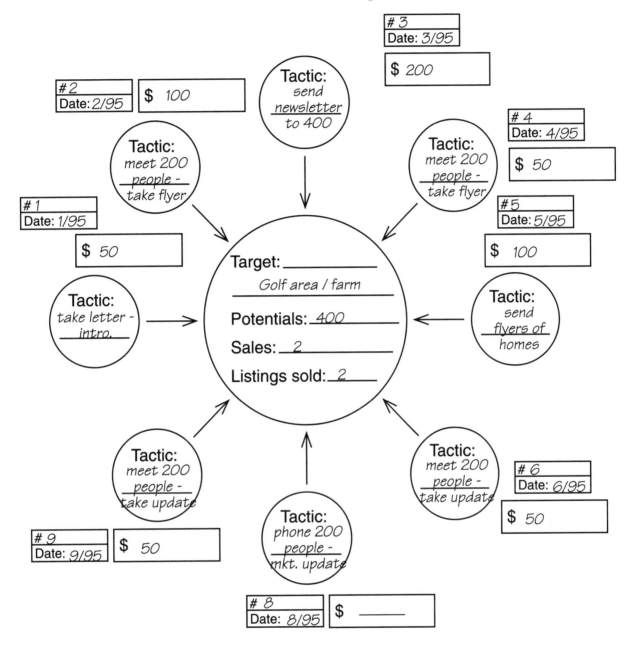

Total tactical impact (number of in-person/telephone): _1,000_ (transfer to Figure 6.6.)

Total budget for this market: $ _600_ . Add this budget to your total marketing budget.

Main messages: *I understand your needs.*
I am area expert - market updates.
My successes in area (flyers, testimonials).   *Ask for leads.*

Create Business-Producing
Tactics for Your Target Market

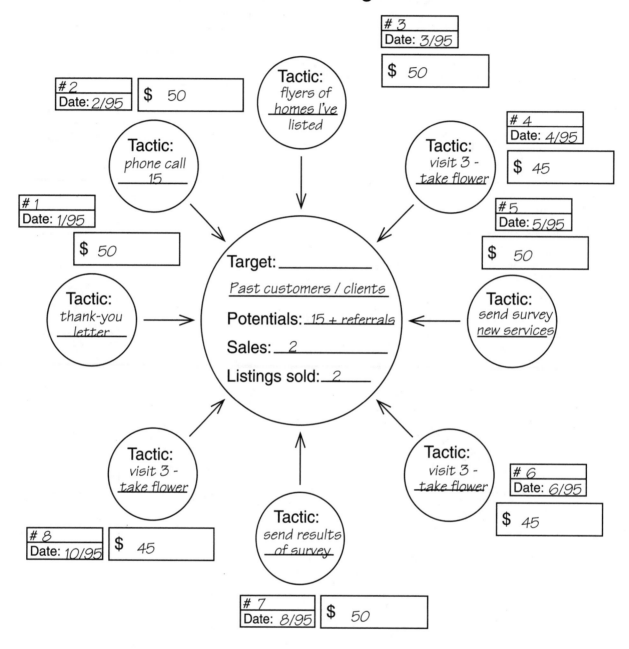

Total tactical impact (number of in-person/telephone): ___24___ (transfer to Figure 6.6.)

Total budget for this market: $ ___385___ . Add this budget to your total marketing budget.

Main messages: *Thanks*
New service
Referrals?

Create Business-Producing Tactics for Your Target Market

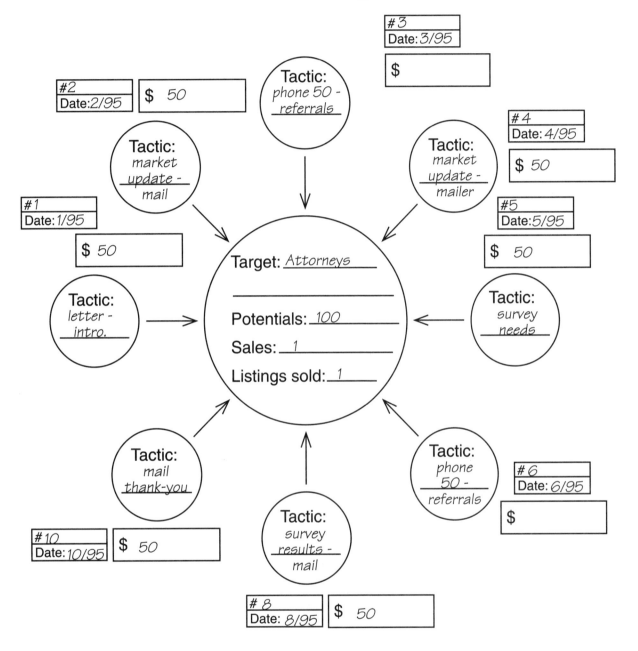

Total tactical impact (number of in-person/telephone): _100_ (transfer to Figure 6.6.)

Total budget for this market: $ _300_ . Add this budget to your total marketing budget.

Main messages: Understand needs - connection/referrals
Professional approach - survey
Professional in field - phone calls

Plan Summary

My main concern at this point in my career is to: _build a solid, growing business around my best sources of business. I'll invest the necessary resources to ensure that my best sources get to know me as a real estate specialist._

My plan will ensure I accomplish this because: _I've picked the right target markets, and am dedicating dollars to them. My consistency and frequency will ensure that, when I call or see these people, I'll get leads._

My overall interest this year is to: _create an image as a residential specialist. I'll create a letter of introduction and a simple mailer format to convey my messages to my target markets._

Tim Johnson

Personal History.   Tim was formerly in the Navy. He has extensive sales experience and has been a sales trainer in another sales field. Tim has lived in the area where he works for three years. He has no relatives in the area. He is single, but planning on getting married in a few months. His future wife is a mortgage officer.

Personal Strengths.   Selling ability and management experience (in the Navy) are Tim's strengths.

Personality Profile.   Tim's sales background developed his abilities as a promoter. He is a natural salesperson, with enough drive to close.

Memberships and Activities.   Tim is a member of the local chapter of the National Speakers' Association. He participates in many volunteer activities in his neighborhood. Recently, Tim has become active in his REALTOR® Association and is a newly elected president of his REALTOR® Council.

Real Estate History.   In his third year in the business, Tim enjoys greater than average success. In his second year, Tim sold 12 homes and 8 of his listings sold. This puts Tim well above the national average of 13.5 for all REALTORS®. His area is a well-defined market of West City, with a population of about 90,000. He specializes in first-time buyers. This market has been hot for first-time buyers in the past year.

A Review of Your Business

Sales ___12___   Listings taken (LT) ___12___

Listings sold (LS) ___8___   % of LT to LS ___66%___

Average time on market for your listings ___30 days___ (Break down by price range if desired)

% of sales price to list price for your listings ___97%___   Number of new listings sold ___0___

Number of resales sold ___7___   Number of resale listings sold ___8___

Number of new homes sold ___1___

Origination of Buyers/Sellers		
	Buyers	Sellers
Reactive Prospecting		
Floor time	2	3
Open houses	4	3
Proactive Prospecting **(Segmented by Target Market)**		
Past customers/clients	3	1
First-time buyers	3	
Move-up buyers		3
Transferees		1
Empty-nesters		
Geographical farm		
Prior business contacts		1
Builders		
Other_____		

Of these sellers, which market gave you the most sold listings?

☞ **Keep exploiting these markets. They're your most effective.**

Analysis: Your Business Strengths and Challenges

Rate yourself as: 1 = Excellent   2 = Very Good

3 = Fair   4 = Needs Improvment

Activity	Rating
Sales	
Finding potential buyers (proactive)	2
Evaluating buying potential	1
Following up with potential buyers	1
Interviewing, qualifying buyers, building rapport	1
Showing properties buyers want to see	1
Helping buyers make buying decisions—closing	1
Evaluating time spent in helping each buyer (too much, not enough?)	2

Activity	Rating
Listing	
Finding potential sellers (proactive)	3
Qualifying sellers	2
Evaluating marketability of product	2
Giving an effective listing presentation	1
Closing for a listing	1
Promoting property	1
Time on market for my properties	2

Activity	Rating
Skills/Operations	
Counseling skills with buyers	1
Negotiating the earnest money agreement	1
Follow-up prior to closing	1
Follow-up after closing—building referral business	2
Distribution plan for marketing myself	2
Telephone skills	1
Open house skills	1

Main goals: *List more properties with a better plan*
                Cutting time on market for my lower-priced properties

Tim Johnson

Vision Statement.   As a residential specialist in West City, I provide services that other agents are unwilling to provide. With my emphasis on satisfied customers and clients, I constantly strive to learn new information that will directly benefit my customers and clients. Through my sales and communication background, I can deliver this information effectively so that my customers and clients can benefit greatly in their real estate decisions. One of my specialty areas is first-time buyers. Through developing special programs, I help them start the process of home ownership with confidence. My objective in my real estate career is to create business relationships that last. My commitment level to real estate is proof that I am in this business for the long-run. My customers and clients reap the benefits of this commitment through building financial security for life.

Personal Operating Expenses

Regular Monthly Payments

House payments (principal, interest, taxes, insurance, condominium fees or rent) • • • $ _____ 700 _____

Car payments (including insurance) • $ _____ 400 _____

Appliance, TV payments • $ _____

Home improvement loan payments • $ _____

Personal loan, credit card payments • $ _____ 100 _____

Health plan payments • $ _____ 100 _____

Life insurance payments • $ _____ 20 _____

Other insurance payments • $ _____

Total • $ _____ 1,320 _____

Household Operating Expenses

Telephone • $ _____ 50 _____

Gas and electricity • $ _____ 150 _____

Water • $ _____ 25 _____

Other household expenses, repairs, maintenance • $ _____ 100 _____

Total • $ _____ 325 _____

Personal Expenses

Clothing, cleaning, laundry • $ _____ 100 _____

Prescription medications • $ _____ 20 _____

Physicians, dentists • $ _____ 10 _____

Education • $ _____ 10 _____

Dues • $ _____ 10 _____

Gifts and contributions • $ _____ 25 _____

Newspapers, magazines, books • $ _____ 25 _____

Auto upkeep and gas (part may go in your real estate budget) • • • • • • • • • • • • • • • $ _____ 25 _____

Children's school tuition • $ _____

Spending money and allowances • $ _____ 200 _____

Miscellaneous • $ _____

Total • $ _____ 425 _____

Food Expenses

Food—at home • $ _____ 200 _____

Food—away from home • $ _____ 200 _____

Total • $ _____ 400 _____

Tax Expenses

Federal and state income taxes • $ _____ 750 _____

Other taxes not included above • $ _____

Total • $ _____ 750 _____

Total Personal Monthly Expenses • $ _____ 3,220 _____

Total Personal Yearly Expenses • $ | 38,640 |

Total Marketing Costs and Analysis of % of Gross Income

Transfer your marketing costs for each target market and listing/selling costs to this sheet.

I.   Target Markets to Generate Business

Past customers/clients	$ 1,500
Geographical farm	$ 1,600
Prior profession	$
Circle of influence	$
Expired listings	$
FSBOs	$
Other - First-time buyers	$ 2,300
Other - Realtors	$ 800
Other	$
Total	$ 6,200

II.   Listing Costs (Cost Per Listing x Number of Listings)

Signs/name signs	$ 25
Display boxes	$ 15
Flyers/brochures	$ 25
Print advertising	$ 25
Mailings	$ 50
Seller gifts	$ 50
Other	$
Total per listing	$ 190
x __24__ listings	
Total	$ 4,560

III.   Other Promotions

Gifts	$ 300
Entertainment	$ 1,200
Personal marketing	
photos	$ 100
brochures	$ 1,800*
graphics	$ 600
printing	$ 400
other	$
Business cards	$ 100
Sponsorships	$ 50
Community service	$ 100
Total	$ 4,650

* Tim is having a brochure done to use when he mails to his target markets, and for his pre-listing/ pre-sales packets.

Total Marketing Expenses $ 15,410

Total Marketing Expense as a % of Income ___16.4___ %
(Marketing expense ÷ gross income)

Professional Development

	Date To Accomplish*	Budget*

Courses, Workshops

_____workshops to develop skill		
✔ Graduate REALTORS'® Institute (GRI)	3/94	200
✔ Certified Residential Specialist (CRS)	8/94	400
_____Certified Real Estate Broker (CRB)		
_____REALTORS'® presentations, workshops		
_____legal updates		
_____technical courses		
✔ hours toward broker's license	12/94	200
_____hours toward continuing education credit		
_____teach real estate course		
_____other		

Books, Tapes

✔ business books bought and read	ongoing	200
✔ audiotapes purchased	ongoing	100
_____videos purchased		
_____study programs purchased		
_____other		

Presentations, Processes, Systems

✔ develop listing presentation marketing manual	2/94	100
_____develop buyers' presentation manual		
_____develop professional portfolio		
_____develop seller qualifying system		
_____develop follow-up systems after the sale		
_____other		

Organizations

✔ become more active in REALTOR® organization	3/94	
_____attend local REALTOR® convention		
✔ attend National REALTOR® Convention	11/94	500
_____join REALTOR® committee		
_____attend company convention		
_____other		
	Total Budget:	$ 1,700

*Add these dates to your business plan calendar. Put the budget items in your operating or marketing budget.

Tim's main objective here is to create a listing strategy to ensure he meets his listing goals. Also, he's found being an active member in the Realtors® organization brings him "leads."

Systems/Mechanical/Labor Checklist

Choose from the following areas the systems and support you want to plan for this year.

	*Date To Accomplish**	*Budget**
Mechanical		
✔ buy a computer, printer	*2/94*	*2,000*
buy a typewriter		
✔ purchase software programs	*2/94*	*800*
purchase computer hardware		
take lessons on computers		
get voicemail, pager		
purchase car phone		
purchase fax machine		
purchase multiple listing service at home		
other		
Labor		
✔ hire assistant	*1/94*	*10,000*
hire mailing service		
other		
Home Office		
office furniture		
office supplies		
fax		
computer/printer		
other		
	Total Budget:	*$ 12,800*

*Put these dates in your business plan calendar. Add these budget items to your operating budget.

Tim will invest in his business this year so he can manage contacts to grow his business.

Your Real Estate Budget
Real Estate Operating Expenses

	Yearly	Monthly
Total marketing budget	$ 15,410	$ 1,284
Professional fees (REALTORS®, MLS)	$ 1,200	$ 100
Business car expenses (gas, oil, tools, repair)	$ 1,800	$ 150
Communications expenses (pager, phone)	$ 1,200	$ 100
Labor/mechanical (from systems worksheet)	$ 12,800	$ 1,067
Professional development (from worksheet)	$ 1,700	$ 142
Supplies	$ 1,200	$ 100
Business insurance	$ 240	$ 20
Legal fees	$ 400	$ 33
Licenses, permits	$ 100	$ 8
Other	$	$
Total	$ 36,050	$ 3,004

Deciding the Profit You Want

Total dollars from Personal Operating Expenses   *$ 38,640*

Total dollars from Real Estate Operating Expenses   *36,050*

Dreams/fun *- getting married*   *4,000*

    Total $ needed to cover total expenses   *78,690*

    Desired profit   *15,000*

    Grand total of dollars you want to earn   *$ 93,690*

Overall Objectives

Name: _Tim Johnson_ Office: _Contact Realty_

Date Completed: _11/93_ For Year: _1994_

Your average commission per sale/listing sold (S/LS) = $ _2,600_

Your past year's ratio of sales written to sales closed _98_ % Your past year's ratio of LT/LS= _66_ %

Your next year's desired ratio _90_ % Your next year's ratio of listings sold to sales _60_ %

Listings:

Number of listings taken (units) _24_

Number of listings sold (units) _21_ x average commission = $ _54,600_ – sales fails ($ ——） = $ _54,600_
net income

Sales:

Number of sales (units) _15_ x average commission = $ _39,000_ – sales fails ($2,600) = $ _36,400_
net income

Referrals out:

Number of referrals (units) _10_ x average commission = $ _4,000_ – sales fails ($ ——） = $ _4,000_
net income

Totals:

Total net revenue units + (LS/S) = | _35_ | Total net commissions paid = $ | _95,000_ |

L = Listing * paid in that year
LS = Listing Sold + a revenue unit = a listing sold or a sale
S = Sale

Setting Objectives for Sales Effectiveness

Of all the areas that you analyzed and want to change and/or improve, which are the most important to you to increase your business effectiveness?

☑ Change ratio of listings taken to listings sold from _66_ % to _90_ %.

☑ Change ratio of listings sold to sales from _40_ % to _60_ %.

☑ Change listing time on market from _30_ average days to _20_ average days.

☑ Increase average commission by changing price range for listings from $ _130,000_ to $ _160,000_ .

☑ Change price range for sales to increase average commission from $ _2,300_ to $ _2,600_ .

☐ To reduce number of showings per sale to _____.

☐ Change ratio of listing presentations to listings that sell from _____ % to _____ %.

☑ Switch from _50_ % proactive methods to find buyers/sellers to _75_ %.

These priorities for your overall sales strategy will provide the basis for your marketing and professional development plans.

Choose Your Target Markets

1. Fill in the top portion of each circle with a name of a potential target (past customers and clients, geographical farm, FSBO, expired listings, certain professions, etc.).

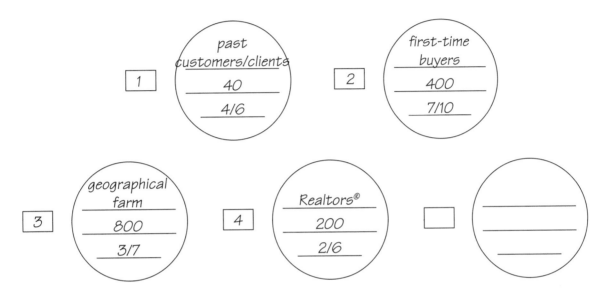

2. Estimate the number of potential contacts in each market by filling the middle blank in each circle (prospecting).

3. Estimate the number of listings sold and sales derived from this market by filling in the bottom portion of the circle.

4. Prioritize the importance of these markets to you by numbering the market in the box (#1 is your best market).

Example:

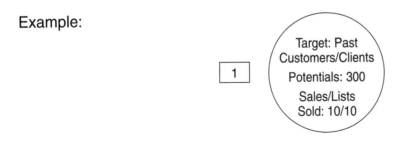

Because Tim has great sales skills, he'll rely on open houses and floor time to bring him six listings.

Past customers/clients includes referrals to them.

First-time buyers becomes #3 because Tim wants to change his business to more listings and less sales. To do that, he adds a geographical farm. He also adds Realtors®, since he's found his activities in his Realtor® organization can bring him "leads."

Create Business-Producing
Tactics for Your Target Market

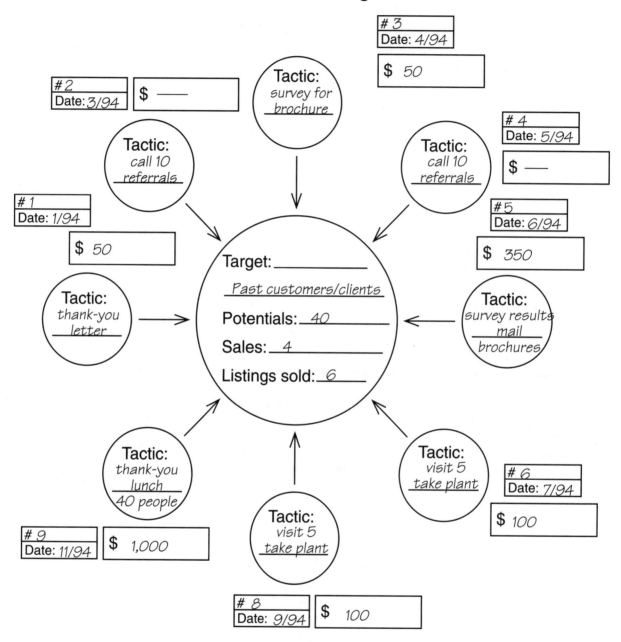

Total tactical impact (number of in-person/telephone): _70_ (transfer to Figure 6.6.)

Total budget for this market: $ _1,650_ . Add this budget to your total marketing budget.

Tim spends more money per potential on this market, because he knows he'll get better long-term results.

Create Business-Producing Tactics for Your Target Market

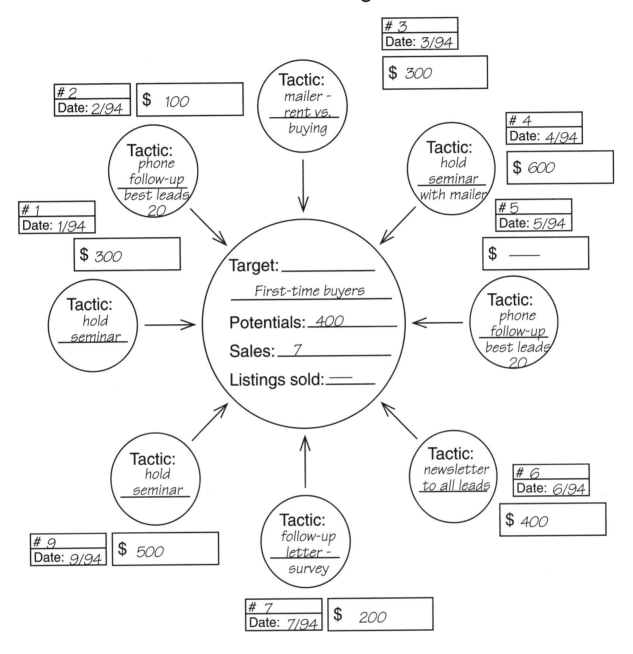

Total tactical impact (number of in-person/telephone): __400__ (transfer to Figure 6.6.)

Total budget for this market: $ __2,400__ . Add this budget to your total marketing budget.

Tim also uses press releases prior to and after each seminar to increase his visibility. He works with a loan officer and a state program to get the best presentation. By investing in first-time buyers, he's laying groundwork to move into higher priced ranges.

Create Business-Producing
Tactics for Your Target Market

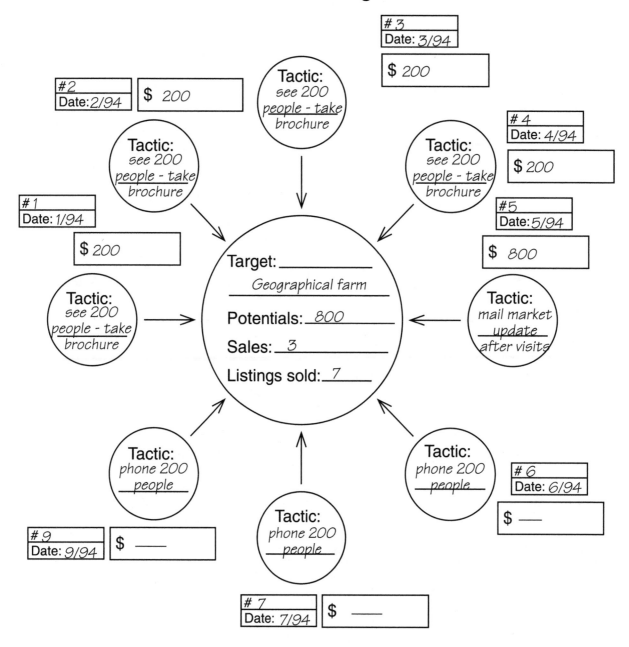

Total tactical impact (number of in-person/telephone): _1,600_ (transfer to Figure 6.6.)

Total budget for this market: $ _1,600_ . Add this budget to your total marketing budget.

Create Business-Producing Tactics for Your Target Market

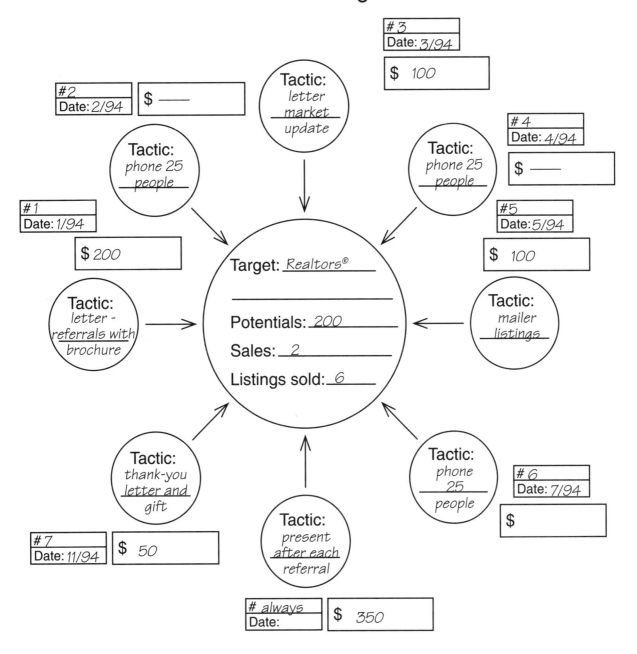

Total tactical impact (number of in-person/telephone): ___275___ (transfer to Figure 6.6.)

Total budget for this market: $ ___800___ . Add this budget to your total marketing budget.

Tim sees Realtors® at all Realtor® functions. Tim knows Realtors® need someone to refer to. He invests in this market for long-term results.

Plan Summary

My main concern at this point in my career is to: manage my contacts
more effectively, so I can grow my career. To manage my time, I need
to list more and sell less.

My plan will ensure I accomplish this because: I'll hire an assistant and
invest in a computer. I'll target my best sources of business to ensure
that I grow my business right.

My overall interest this year is to: list more and sell less. Maintain my
first-time buyer base, but move into higher-priced homes and listings.
Expand my image by creating a brochure and promoting to Realtors®
for referral business.

Planning Worksheets

Market/Business Review

The Big Picture
Market Analysis
Analyzing Your Company/Your Office
Analyzing Your Competition
Company Analysis/Market Strategy
A Review of Your Business
Analysis: Your Business Strengths and Challenges
Personal Internal Analysis

Vision

Creating Your Vision

Objectives

Life Goals
Personal Operating Expenses
Your Real Estate Budget: Real Estate Operating Expenses
Total Marketing Costs and Analysis of % of Gross Income
Deciding the Profit You Want
Overall Objectives
Time Line: Annual Production Plan in Units
Setting Objectives for Sales Effectiveness
Activities, Expenses, Results, Profits
Plan Summary

Marketing

Expanding Your Business: Choose Your Target Markets
Create Business-Producing Tactics for a Particular Market
Itemization of Tactics with Dates, Budget
Business Planning Calendar

Professional Development

Professional Development
Systems/Mechanical/Labor Checklist
Support from My Office, Manager and Company

Plan Review

Business Plan Three-Month Review

The Big Picture

Evaluate these factors as you believe they impact your market:

+ Positive Impact
- Negative Impact
o No Impact

	Rating	Comments
National Economy Politics Environment Employment National resources **Local** Economy Politics Environment Mortgage availability Consumer interest rates Housing availability Natural resources Schools Community services Employment		

Market Analysis

	This Year	Last Year
Overall		
Total number of homes available (listed)		
Total number of homes sold		
New		
Number of homes available (listed)		
Number of homes sold		
Resale		
Number of homes available (listed)		
Number of homes sold		

By Price Range: Homes Available	This Year	Last Year
0–99		
100–150		
151–200		
201–300		
301–400		
401–500		
over 501		

Analyzing Your Company/Your Office

Rate your company / office in these areas:

1 = Highest   2 = Above Average

3 = Average   4 = Needs Improving

	Rating	Comments

Company
    Image/reputation
    Management communication
    Marketing programs
    Training
    Business producing programs
    Team awareness
    Policies
    Creativity
    Compensation
    Planning
 	
Office
    Management
    Support—staff/mechanical
    Team awareness
    Training
    Creativity
    Image
    Working conditions
    Planning
    Communications		

Analyzing Your Competition

Best Company Competitors

S = strength W = weakness Names →	S	W	S	W	S	W	S	W	S	W	S	W
Overall marketing strategy												
Competition for listings												
Competition for buyers												
Image/reputation												
Quality of associates												
Rate overall competitive position												

Best Agent Competitors

S = strength W = weakness Names →	S	W	S	W	S	W	S	W	S	W	S	W
Overall marketing strategy												
Competition for listings												
Competition for buyers												
Image reputation												
Quality of associates												
Rate overall competitive position												

Company Analysis/Market Strategy

Overall analysis of the market conditions:

_____

_____

_____

_____

Overall analysis of office position in the market:

Strengths

_____

_____

_____

Challenges

_____

_____

Competitor evaluation:

Main competitors

_____

_____

Strengths

_____

_____

Company/office strategy for the next year:

Markets to capture

_____

_____

Promotional moves planned

_____

Other:

_____

_____

A Review of Your Business

Sales _____   Listings taken (LT) _____

Listings sold (LS) _____   % of LT to LS _____

Average time on market for your listings _____ (Break down by price range if desired)

% of sales price to list price for your listings _____   Number of new listings sold _____

Number of resales sold _____   Number of resale listings sold _____

Number of new homes sold _____

Origination of Buyers/Sellers	Buyers	Sellers
Reactive Prospecting		
Floor time		
Open houses		
Proactive Prospecting (Segmented by Target Market)		
Past customers/clients		
First-time buyers		
Move-up buyers		
Transferees		
Empty-nesters		
Geographical farm		
Prior business contacts		
Builders		
Other_____		

Of these sellers, which market gave you the most sold listings?

☞   **Keep exploiting these markets. They're your most effective.**

Analysis: Your Business Strengths and Challenges

Rate yourself as: 1 = Excellent   2 = Very Good

3 = Fair   4 = Needs Improvment

Activity	Rating
Sales	
Finding potential buyers (proactive)	
Evaluating buying potential	
Following up with potential buyers	
Interviewing, qualifying buyers, building rapport	
Showing properties buyers want to see	
Helping buyers make buying decisions—closing	
Evaluating time spent in helping each buyer (too much, not enough?)	

Activity	Rating
Listing	
Finding potential sellers (proactive)	
Qualifying sellers	
Evaluating marketability of product	
Giving an effective listing presentation	
Closing for a listing	
Promoting property	
Time on market for my properties	

Activity	Rating
Skills/Operations	
Counseling skills with buyers	
Negotiating the earnest money agreement	
Follow-up prior to closing	
Follow-up after closing—building referral business	
Distribution plan for marketing myself	
Telephone skills	
Open house skills	

Personal Internal Analysis

Analysis of your attitude toward your business:

_____
_____
_____

Barriers that deterred you from attaining your business goals last year:

_____
_____
_____

Personal challenges—family:

_____
_____
_____

Possible solutions:

_____
_____
_____

Personal challenges—other:

_____
_____
_____

Possible solutions:

_____
_____
_____

Recognized motivators in my past:

_____
_____
_____

How I can motivate myself to address the barriers and challenges above:

_____
_____
_____

Creating Your Vision

What you do: _____
_____
_____
_____

Where you sell: _____
_____
_____
_____

What you sell (properties): _____
_____
_____
_____

What you specialize in (your target properties, buyers, sellers): _____
_____
_____
_____

What you don't/won't sell—geographical types of sellers, buyers, properties, other kinds of real estate (this is to help you refine your focus; it is not for publication): _____
_____
_____

Your business values: _____
_____
_____

Talents, specialties, competencies you bring from your other fields: _____
_____
_____

Benefits: _____
_____
_____
_____

How you are different from other real estate people: _____
_____
_____
_____

Life Goals

You are now retired. Describe your ideal life: _____

_____

_____

_____

You are retired looking back over your life. Your comments: _____

_____

_____

_____

You are listening in as friends, business associates, customers and clients discuss you. What are they saying? _____

_____

_____

_____

What do you want to be when you grow up? _____

_____

_____

_____

How can real estate assure you of becoming that person? _____

_____

_____

You have $5 million. How will you spend it? _____

_____

_____

Personal Operating Expenses

Regular Monthly Payments

House payments (principal, interest, taxes, insurance, condominium fees or rent) • • • $ _____

Car payments (including insurance) • $ _____

Appliance, TV payments • $ _____

Home improvement loan payments • $ _____

Personal loan, credit card payments • $ _____

Health plan payments • $ _____

Life insurance payments • $ _____

Other insurance payments • $ _____

Total • $ _____

Household Operating Expenses

Telephone • $ _____

Gas and electricity • $ _____

Water • $ _____

Other household expenses, repairs, maintenance • $ _____

Total • $ _____

Personal Expenses

Clothing, cleaning, laundry • $ _____

Prescription medications • $ _____

Physicians, dentists • $ _____

Education • $ _____

Dues • $ _____

Gifts and contributions • $ _____

Newspapers, magazines, books • $ _____

Auto upkeep and gas (part may go in your real estate budget) • • • • • • • • • • • • • • • • $ _____

Children's school tuition • $ _____

Spending money and allowances • $ _____

Miscellaneous • $ _____

Total • $ _____

Food Expenses

Food—at home • $ _____

Food—away from home • $ _____

Total • $ _____

Tax Expenses

Federal and state income taxes • $ _____

Other taxes not included above • $ _____

Total • $ _____

Total Personal Monthly Expenses • $ _____

Total Personal Yearly Expenses • $ ⌐_____⌐

Your Real Estate Budget
Real Estate Operating Expenses

	Yearly	*Monthly*
Total marketing budget	$ _____	$ _____
Professional fees (REALTORS®, MLS)	$ _____	$ _____
Business car expenses (gas, oil, tools, repair)	$ _____	$ _____
Communications expenses (pager, phone)	$ _____	$ _____
Labor/mechanical (from systems worksheet)	$ _____	$ _____
Professional development (from worksheet)	$ _____	$ _____
Supplies	$ _____	$ _____
Business insurance	$ _____	$ _____
Legal fees	$ _____	$ _____
Licenses, permits	$ _____	$ _____
Other	$ _____	$ _____
Total	$ _____	$ _____

Total Marketing Costs and Analysis of % of Gross Income

Transfer your marketing costs for each target market and listing/selling costs to this sheet.

I.   Target Markets to Generate Business

               Past customers/clients $ _____

               Geographical farm $ _____

               Prior profession $ _____

               Circle of influence $ _____

               Expired listings $ _____

               FSBOs $ _____

               Other $ _____

               Other $ _____

               Other $ _____

                   Total $ _____

II.   Listing Costs (Cost Per Listing x Number of Listings)

               Signs/name signs $ _____

               Display boxes $ _____

               Flyers/brochures $ _____

               Print advertising $ _____

               Mailings $ _____

               Seller gifts $ _____

               Other $ _____

               Total per listing $ _____

               x _____ listings   _____

                   Total $ _____

III.   Other Promotions

               Gifts $ _____

               Entertainment $ _____

               Personal marketing

                   photos $ _____

                   brochures $ _____

                   graphics $ _____

                   printing $ _____

                   other $ _____

               Business cards $ _____

               Sponsorships $ _____

               Community service $ _____

                   Total $ _____

Total Marketing Expenses $ _____

Total Marketing Expense as a % of Income _____ %
(Marketing expense ÷ gross income)

Deciding the Profit You Want

Total dollars from Personal Operating Expenses   _____

Total dollars from Real Estate Operating Expenses   _____

Dreams/fun   _____

    Total $ needed to cover total expenses   [_____]

    Desired profit   _____

    Grand total of dollars you want to earn   [_____]

Overall Objectives

Name: _____

Office: _____

Date Completed: _____

For Year: _____

Your average commission per sale/listing sold (S/LS) = $ _____

Your past year's ratio of sales written to sales closed _____ %   Your past year's ratio of LT/LS = _____ %

Your next year's desired ratio _____ %   Your next year's ratio of listings sold to sales _____ %

Listings:

Number of listings taken (units) _____

Number of listings sold (units) _____ x average commission = $ _____ – sales fails ($ _____) = $ _____ net income

Sales:

Number of sales (units) _____ x average commission = $ _____ – sales fails ($ _____) = $ _____ net income

Referrals out:

Number of referrals (units) _____ x average commission = $ _____ – sales fails ($ _____) = $ _____ net income

Totals:

Total net revenue units + (LS/S) = _____   Total net commissions paid = $ _____ *

L = Listing
LS = Listing Sold
S = Sale

* paid in that year
+ a revenue unit = a listing sold or a sale

Timeline:
Annual Production Plan in Units

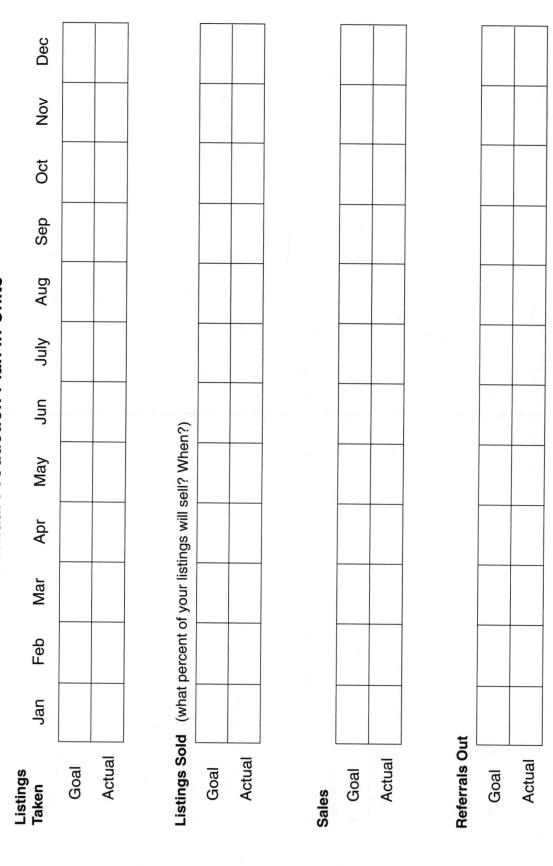

Listings Taken

	Jan	Feb	Mar	Apr	May	Jun	July	Aug	Sep	Oct	Nov	Dec
Goal												
Actual												

Listings Sold (what percent of your listings will sell? When?)

Goal												
Actual												

Sales

Goal												
Actual												

Referrals Out

Goal												
Actual												

Setting Objectives for Sales Effectiveness

Of all the areas that you analyzed and want to change and/or improve, which are the most important to you to increase your business effectiveness?

☐ Change ratio of listings taken to listings sold from_____ % to _____ %.

☐ Change ratio of listings sold to sales from _____ % to _____ %.

☐ Change listing time on market from _____ average days to _____ average days.

☐ Increase average commission by changing price range for listings from $ _____

to $ _____ .

☐ Change price range for sales to increase average commission from $ _____ to

$ _____ .

☐ Reduce number of showings per sale to _____ .

☐ Change ratio of listing presentations to listings that sell from _____ % to _____ %.

☐ Switch from _____ % proactive methods to find buyers/sellers to _____ %.

These priorities for your overall sales strategy will provide the basis for your marketing and professional development plans.

Activities, Expenses, Results, Profits

1. Estimate your activities and when they will create income. Start with face-to-face contacts.

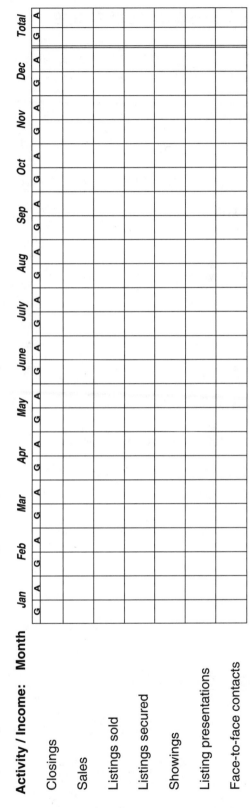

Activity / Income: Month	Jan		Feb		Mar		Apr		May		June		July		Aug		Sep		Oct		Nov		Dec		Total	
	G	A	G	A	G	A	G	A	G	A	G	A	G	A	G	A	G	A	G	A	G	A	G	A	G	A
Closings																										
Sales																										
Listings sold																										
Listings secured																										
Showings																										
Listing presentations																										
Face-to-face contacts																										

2. Tally your expenses per month. Log in your projected earnings and "paids."

Business expenses											
Earned income (written)											
Paid income (closed)											
Profit per month											
Profit (year-to-date)											

G = Goal
A = Actual

Reprinted with permission: *Up and Running in 30 Days*, © 1993 Carla Cross Seminars. Published by Carla Cross Seminars, Issaquah, WA. All rights reserved.

Plan Summary

My main concern at this point in my career is to: _____

_____

_____

_____

_____

My plan will ensure I accomplish this because: _____

_____

_____

_____

_____

My overall interest this year is to: _____

_____

_____

_____

_____

Choose Your Target Markets

1.   Fill in the top portion of each circle with a name of a potential target (past customers and clients, geographical farm, FSBO, expired listings, certain professions, etc.).

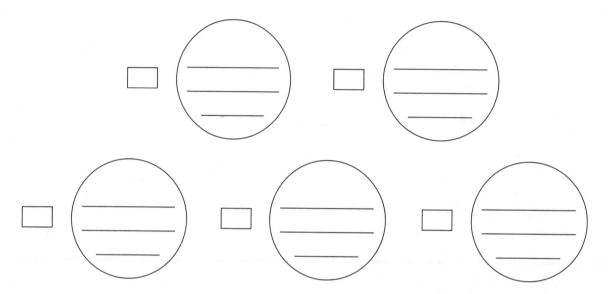

2.   Estimate the number of potential contacts in each market by filling the middle blank in each circle (prospecting).

3.   Estimate the number of listings sold and sales derived from this market by filling in the bottom portion of the circle.

4.   Prioritize the importance of these markets to you by numbering the market in the box (#1 is your best market).

Example:

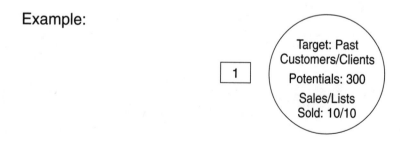

Create Business-Producing
Tactics for Your Target Market

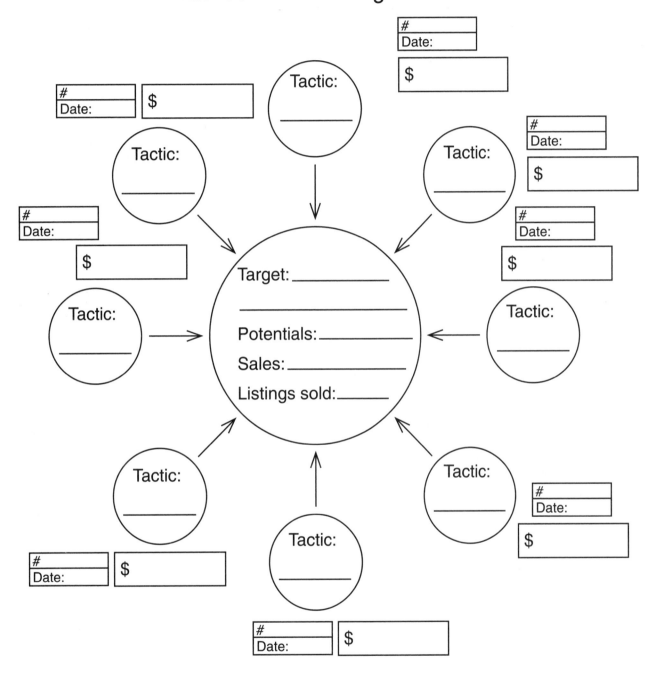

Total tactical impact (number of in-person/telephone): _____ (transfer to Figure 6.6.)

Total budget for this market: $ _____ . Add this budget to your total marketing budget.

Itemization of Tactics with Dates, Budget

Name your target market. Put your tactics in order of the dates to be accomplished. Assign work to be accomplished in each tactic. Add your budget figure. Then, tally your total budget from this target market. Put the total budget on your marketing budget worksheet.

Target Market: _____

Tactic*	Assigned To	To Be Done By	Budget

*Use tactical planning worksheet to create mini-plan for each of your tactics, if needed.

Business Planning Calendar

Month _____

Goals: Prospecting
Listing presentations
Listings
Showings
Sales
Listings sold

\# _____
\# _____
\# _____
\# _____
\# _____
\# _____

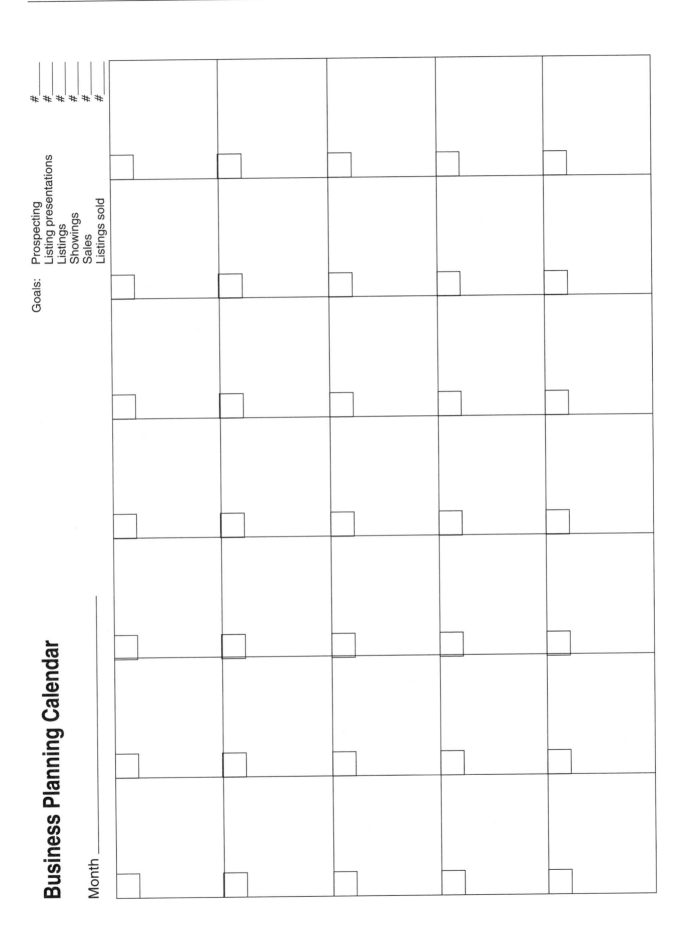

Professional Development

Date To Accomplish*   *Budget**

Courses, Workshops

_____workshops to develop skill
_____Graduate Realtors'® Institute (GRI)
_____Certified Residential Specialist (CRS)
_____Certified Real Estate Broker (CRB)
_____Realtors'® presentations, workshops
_____legal updates
_____technical courses
_____hours toward broker's license
_____hours toward continuing education credit
_____teach real estate course
_____other

Books, Tapes

_____business books bought and read
_____audiotapes purchased
_____videos purchased
_____study programs purchased
_____other

Presentations, Processes, Systems

_____develop listing presentation marketing manual
_____develop buyers' presentation manual
_____develop professional portfolio
_____develop seller qualifying system
_____develop follow-up systems after the sale
_____other

Organizations

_____become more active in Realtor® organization
_____attend local Realtor® convention
_____attend National Realtor® Convention
_____join Realtor® committee
_____attend company convention
_____other

Total Budget:

*Add these dates to your business plan calendar. Put the budget items in your operating or marketing budget.

Systems/Mechanical/Labor Checklist

Choose from the following areas the systems and support you want to plan for this year.

Date To Accomplish*   **Budget***

Mechanical

_____buy a computer, printer
_____buy a typewriter
_____purchase software programs
_____purchase computer hardware
_____take lessons on computers
_____get voicemail, pager
_____purchase car phone
_____purchase fax machine
_____purchase multiple listing service at home
_____other

Labor

_____hire assistant
_____hire mailing service
_____other

Home Office

_____office furniture
_____office supplies
_____fax
_____computer/printer
_____other

Total Budget:

*Put these dates in your business plan calendar. Add these budget items to your operating budget.

Support from My Office, Manager and Company

Materials/Resources: _____

_____

_____

_____

Operations: _____

_____

_____

_____

Management Consultation: _____

_____

_____

_____

Training: _____

_____

_____

_____

Other: _____

_____

_____

_____

_____

_____

_____

_____

_____

Business Plan Three-Month Review

Quarterly goals: Listings Taken _____   For months _____

Listings Sold _____

Sales _____

1.   Management by the Numbers

My analysis of my activities/results to date: _____

_____

My analysis of my expenses/profitability to date: _____

_____

Adjustments I need to make: _____

_____

2.   Marketing

My analysis of my results from specific target markets: _____

_____

My analysis of my specific promotional tactics effectiveness: _____

_____

Changes I need to make: _____

_____

3.   Professional Development

My analysis of my accomplishments: _____

_____

Adjustments I need to make: _____

_____

4.   The Big Picture

Does my stated focus match the results of my activities and my overall business

objectives for this year? _____ Adjustments I need to make:_____

_____

_____

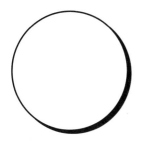

References

Developing Your Business

How about a Career in Real Estate? Carla Cross. Chicago: Real Estate Education Company, a division of Dearborn Publishing, Inc., 1993. Endorsed and recommended by the Real Estate Brokerage Managers' Council.

Up and Running in 30 Days. Carla Cross Seminars, 1993. 150-page handbook explains the concepts of planning by the numbers, how to set goals and keep track of achievements. Worksheets and explanations of sales calls and sales skills. Six audiotapes provide step-by-step guidance and role-plays of sales calls and sales skills. Endorsed and recommended by the Real Estate Brokerage Managers' Council, an affiliate of the National Association of REALTORS®. Carla Cross Seminars, 1070 Idylwood Dr. S.W., Issaquah, WA 98027. 206-392-6914.

Delegating

Multiply Your Success with Real Estate Assistants: How To Hire, Train and Manage Your Assistant, Featuring over 85 Ready-To-Use Forms. Monica Reynolds. Chicago: Real Estate Education Company, a division of Dearborn Publishing, Inc., 1994.

Systematizing: Software

The following programs for real estate salespeople are endorsed by the Residential Sales Council:

Howard and Friends, a real estate productivity software package. 505-525-9199.

The Real Estate Specialist, marketing tool for tracking customers and properties. 818-952-1000.

Realty 2000, an integrated system—offering full customer and propery databases, daily planner, time management, mail merge, labels, envelopes—prepares buyer/seller financial reports. 800-421-3069.

Residential Trans/Act, a real estate specific data base template sold in conjunction with ACT! contact management program. 303-321-3341.

Top Producer 4.2, a sales and marketing program designed for high-volume agents. 800-444-8570.

Marketing Concepts

How To Win Customers and Keep Them for Life. Michael Lebouef, Ph.D. New York: Berkley, 1989.

The Manager's Guide to Real Estate Marketing. Hal Kahn. Chicago: Real Estate Brokerage Managers' Council, REALTORS® National Marketing Institute, an affiliate of the National Association of REALTORS®, 1989. 800-621-8738.

Positioning: The Battle for Your Mind. Al Ries and Jack Trout. New York: McGraw-Hill, revised edition, 1986.

Total Customer Service. William H. Davidow and Bro Uttal. New York: Harper and Row, 1989.

Personal Marketing Tactics

1992 Residential Sales Council Marketing Tools Yearbook, best personal promotional pieces in the country. CRS Council, 1993. 800-852-7592.

Personal Promotion. Dave Beson. Dave Beson Seminars, 1989, 8140 Flying Cloud Dr., Suite 108, Eden Prairie, MN 55344. 612-941-2560.

The following books are endorsed by the Real Estate Brokerage Managers' Council:

Persuasive Presentations. Ed Hall, CRB, CRS. Benchmarks for Success, Ltd., 1992, 1 S. 510 Domartin Place, Winfield, IL 60190. 708-352-4840.

The Power of PR. Ed Hall, CRB, CRS. Benchmarks for Success, Ltd.,1992, 1 S. 510 Domartin Place, Winfield, IL 60190. 708-352-4840.

Techniques for the Talented. Ed Hall, CRB, CRS. Benchmarks for Success, Ltd., 1993, 1 S. 510 Domartin Place, Winfield, IL 60190. 708-352-4840.

Total Quality Management (for Self-Management)

Bringing Total Quality to Sales. Cas Welch and Peter Geissler. Milwaukee: ASQC Quality Press, 1992. 800-248-1946.

Making Quality Work: A Leadership Guide for the Results-Driven Manager. George Labovitz. New York: HarperBusiness, 1993. 212-207-7000.

Putting Total Quality Management to Work: What TQM Means, How To Use It. Marshall Sashkin and Kenneth Kiser. San Francisco: Berrett-Koehler, 1993. 800-929-2929.

Educational Resources for Business Planning

Certified Real Estate Broker (CRB). A comprehensive series of one-day courses, focusing on the various aspects of real estate management, including the latest management techniques applied to real estate. Course number 449 titled, "Implementing High-Profit Agent Business Planning To Increase Office Profitability," shows managers how to manage the agent business planning process. For information on the courses and designation, write to the Real Estate Brokerage Managers' Council, 430 N. Michigan Ave., Chicago, IL 60611. 800-621-8738.

Certified Residential Specialist (CRS). A series of seven courses, any three of which provide partial qualification to earn the CRS designation. CRS introduced a business planning course in 1994, named *Business Development for the Residential Specialist* (course number 200). These courses are offered nationally. For information on the courses and the designation, write to the Residential Sales Council, 430 N. Michigan Ave., Chicago, IL 60611. 800-462-8841.

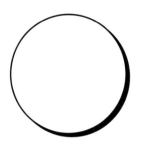

Index